TEARING STRIPES OFF ZEBRAS

Forty Years of Women Writing in Ireland

By this creature drowsing now in every house,
The same lion who tore stripes
Once off zebras, who now sleeps
Small beside the coals and may
On a red letter day
Catch a mouse.

from Eavan Boland's 'Ode to Suburbia'

Nessa O'Mahony

editor

TEARING STRIPES OFF ZEBRAS

Forty Years of Women Writing in Ireland

ARLEN
HOUSE

Tearing Stripes off Zebras

is published in 2023 by
ARLEN HOUSE
42 Grange Abbey Road
Baldoyle
Dublin D13 A0F3
Ireland
Email: arlenhouse@gmail.com
www.arlenhouse.ie

ISBN 978–1–85132–300–5, *paperback*
ISBN 978–1–85132–310–4, *limited edition hardback*

International distribution
SYRACUSE UNIVERSITY PRESS
621 Skytop Road, Suite 110
Syracuse
New York 13244–5290
USA
Email: supress@syr.edu
www.syracuseuniversitypress.syr.edu

Typesetting by Arlen House
Copy-editing by Robert Doran

cover artwork:
'Wet Night in Goatstown' by Mary Burke
is reproduced courtesy of the artist

LOTTERY FUNDED

CONTENTS

In Memory of Eavan Boland
1944–2020

Current members
Ivy Bannister
Sheila Barrett
Mary Rose Callaghan
Catherine Dunne
Celia de Fréine
Shauna Gilligan
Phyl Herbert
Patricia Hickey
Liz McManus
Lia Mills
Sara Mullen
Patsy J. Murphy
Éilís Ní Dhuibhne
Clairr O'Connor
Máiríde Woods

Former members
Louise C. Callaghan
Susan Connolly
Colette Connor
Phil Feighery
Antonia Hart
Joan Flanagan Leech
Antoinette McCarthy
Ann McKay
Marilyn McLaughlin
Helena Nolan
Mary O'Donnell
Beth O'Halloran
Anne Roper
Breda Wall Ryan
Susan Schreibman
Monica Strina
Dolores Walshe

Rialtas Áitiúil Éireann
Local Government Ireland

Clár Éire Ildánach
Creative Ireland
Programme

Comhairle Contae County Council

Catherine Gallagher and Cllr Denis O'Callaghan

FOREWORD

The vision of Dún Laoghaire-Rathdown public libraries is of a progressive, vibrant service that is attractive, inclusive and accessible to our communities, enabling them to connect with one another, collaborate, create and learn. As part of this mission, words, the making of them, the reading of them and the sharing of them, have always been of central importance. We aspire for our libraries to be places of reading discovery and to provide opportunities for our communities to access collections that excite and energise. Dún Laoghaire Rathdown has a rich literary and cultural heritage, it has been a home and an inspiration to many writers and poets who have left their mark.

Words enrich our lives and as such we continue to celebrate and encourage writing and authors/illustrators through Residencies, Adopt an Author programmes, creative writing groups, book clubs, author events, Poetry at the LexIcon and a whole myriad of events to connect authors/poets with existing and new audiences.

We also have the Irish Author Collection on Level 5, dlr LexIcon. This is an exciting initiative whereby dlr Libraries host a comprehensive collection of Irish authors in two sequences, one a reference collection and the other a lending collection, both of which are invaluable for researchers, writers, students and the general public.

Without words, we simply could not exist. And with them, in their various shapes and incarnations, we are enriched beyond measure. As such we continually try to develop opportunities to engage with writers, to support them and find ways of bringing their work to a wider audience.

That's why, the Caothaoirleach and I were delighted to accept the invitation to write a few words in preface to this splendid anthology of new writing by women who are current or past members of WEB, the writers' group that emerged from the Women's Education Bureau workshops organised by Arlen House in the 1980s, facilitated by Eavan Boland. Eavan, to whom this volume is dedicated, was of course one of our finest poets and a writer who spent so much of her writing life in the Dún Laoghaire Rathdown suburb of Dundrum, where she married and raised her family, and where she set about shaping a new type of poetry that could capture the extraordinary beauty in the everyday suburban lives of the men and women who surrounded her.

Visible from the LexIcon is the granite stone harbour she so beautifully describes in her poem 'The Harbour', which she tells us was 'made by art and force./And called Kingstown and afterwards Dún Laoghaire./And holds the sea behind its barrier'. Eavan was a writer of place, and everywhere her precise eye settled, whether it was in the garden of a housing estate in Dundrum or a children's playground in a south Dublin park, resulted in poetry that perfectly evoked the experience of being in that place. But she remained acutely aware of the historical and social forces that had shaped that place.

Towards the end of the poem 'The Harbour' she tells us that 'I am your citizen'. For Eavan Boland, and for the writers who have submitted their wonderful work to this anthology, that citizenship means that writing is also 'made by art and force'. They are aware of the need to capture experience but also to explore its significance to the world in which we now live.

An Caothaoirleach, Cllr O'Callaghan also hopes that you, like him, will enjoy the huge variety of work included in this lovely volume, written by women who have been honing their crafts over four decades. They have taken huge strides since those early days attending workshops or writers' groups, shyly sharing their drafts and offering feedback to their fellow members, and have accumulated many awards and recognition along the way. We applaud their determination to continue to develop their craft, and their generosity in sharing the results of their labours with readers. We look forward to seeing the anthology on our library shelves and available to borrow for our communities of readers. Hopefully it will inspire others to share their words and stories with new generations of readers and writers.

Catherine Gallagher, County Librarian
Cllr Denis O'Callaghan, Caothaoirleach
Dún Laoghaire-Rathdown County Council

Nessa O'Mahony

INTRODUCTION

For many writers, there is a pivotal moment that dictates the direction their writing takes. It is a moment that either confirms their sense that the written word will help them navigate their way through life and that they have something unique to offer in shaping those words, or else crushes that faith in themselves altogether. Often that moment occurs in a writing workshop or writers' group, and there are many aspiring writers out there who never got further than that first hostile reaction to a draft. Who, worse still, never got the opportunity to share their early, hesitant writing in the first place, and as a result faltered and finally stopped. Those of us who were lucky enough to find that encouragement in small groups of engaging listeners, seated in circles in empty classrooms or at the back of a local library, know how crucial to our developing self confidence and sense of voice that workshop experience is. The contributors to this volume certainly do.

This anthology is made up of writing by women who, at one time or another, took part in a writers' group which emerged in the mid 1980s after some of these contributors attended workshops organised by WEB (the Women's Education Bureau), including the Annual Writers' Workshop for Women, and other workshops held in various venues in Dublin and beyond. WEB was the brainchild of Arlen House founder Catherine Rose, who appointed poet Eavan Boland as Creative Director. As an editor at Arlen House from 1978, Boland did much extraordinary work to develop, mentor and promote Irish women writers. Discussing this work in 1984 she said:

> The majority of women remain closet writers. They are very slow to come forward and pronounce themselves a 'writer'. Instead they remain writing for themselves, without an audience or critical appraisal – the essential framework for a writer's development ... Women are too afraid to send their work out to be judged – they have such a low opinion of their own talent ... Women have found it difficult to fulfil their conceived social role as a wife and mother while being a writer, so they have remained fugitive writers, tied up in their own families, forced to dismiss their own writing in public as just a hobby.

> At the workshops women told me how shy, almost embarrassed, they felt even saying they were writers. That is why I feel it is so important that people such as the Arts Council should begin running closed workshops for women, because many of these women would not have come if the workshops had been open to men. I think the high number of applications shows how badly women need this kind of facility ... We need to get back to basics. We can only have women up in the [Arts Council] bursary lists if we set up the basics to encourage and develop their work. Widespread workshops with creches and basic educational facilities using the vocational and comprehensive network would help. The Arts Council needs to look at this area and consider the responsibility they have to bring out literary excellence (*Irish Times*, 23 November 1984).

Arlen House received over 200 applications for just 20 available spaces in those autumn 1984 workshops. Women travelled from as far as Cape Clear, Galway, Sligo and Waterford for these weekend workshops conducted by Eavan Boland, Clare Boylan and Mary Rose Callaghan. In the same interview Catherine Rose reiterated:

> We're not in the business of promoting women writers just because they're women, and we're not asking the Arts Council to do that either. Our aim is to publish excellence and we'd like to see the Arts Council bringing forth the excellence that lies buried in many talented women writers.

Recently I asked Catherine Rose for her own perspective on those early years:

> Arlen House was established as a feminist book publisher and women grew to have tremendous loyalty to the imprint. We were usually invited to have a presence at feminist gatherings and these, and other fora, gave us direct access to women as readers.
>
> An early initiative, with the objective of encouraging women to write and to present their writing for publication, was a literary awards scheme sponsored by Maxwell House. This, and initiatives such as the once-off Readers and Writers Day in the National Gallery, enabled us to recognise women's eagerness for mediated access – both as writers and as readers – to literature by women.
>
> It came to a stage whereby anything educational and informative that we offered was over-subscribed and it was obvious that women were keen to have access to more than a book publishing enterprise offering occasional workshops. There was evidence of a growing enthusiasm among more and more women for creative writing workshops. We reckoned that the time was right to establish a discrete supportive entity for women writers. Thus was WEB born.
>
> Eavan, of course, was central to all these developments and she facilitated almost all of the early workshops. She was passionate about meeting women's expressed wishes – opportunities to meet both established writers and those who were keen to hone their craft.

The founders of this WEB writers' group initially met at these empowering, transformative workshops. And they have been meeting continuously for almost forty years, making WEB one of the longest-running writing groups in Ireland. The group meets once a month at a city centre location to peer review their work. Over the years, WEB writers and alumni have established highly-successful literary careers, publishing books, having plays and film scripts produced, and winning prestigious literary prizes. Four of the original members still attend the group regularly.

In the aftermath of Eavan Boland's sudden death in 2020, and with the upcoming fortieth anniversary of the group's foundation, it was felt that bringing together an anthology of writing by current and former members would be the best way of paying tribute to the contribution that Eavan Boland made to developing women's writing in Ireland. The editorial team made contact with as many former members as we could find in the short timeframe available to us, and we were delighted with the generosity and enthusiasm of the response.

So here you'll find fiction and poetry, creative non-fiction and drama of the highest calibre. Whilst the subject matter and form varies greatly, there's a recurring attentiveness to the power of the word and its ability to create empathy in the reader.

One senses that Eavan would be very happy with such a legacy. In her famous essay *A Kind of Scar* she quotes American poet and critic Alicia Ostriker's comment that 'where women write strongly as women, it is clear that their intention is to subvert the life and literature they inherit'. The writers included here have all, in one way or another, subverted that inherited tradition, and have taken Eavan's lead in giving women's lives the primacy they deserve in the Irish literary canon.

Ivy Bannister

ROSE AND MISTER FLUFF

Rose is an older woman for whom age is merely a number. Slim, fit and lively, she presents herself with elegant simplicity, her outfit including a dusky pink blouse. As the lights go up, we see her loving a small, invisible dog, whom she's cuddling in her arms. The play, in fact, is addressed to Mister Fluff, who is Rose's best friend. Rose herself provides her dog's dialogue in a quiet but expressive range of doggy intonations. A make-up table with chair, and a cushion for Mister Fluff, provide the set.

I've briefly suggested glosses of the dog's dialogue. Embellishments at the discretion of actress and director.

ROSE (*snuggling*): Who's a bootiful boy, then? G'wan ... give us a ... (*She kisses him*). Mwah! ... Big day, today. A funeral.

Er-uff?

Henry Harring's funeral ... Harring, like herring, only fishier.

Rrurr? (WHO?)

It's a long story.

Ruf-ruf-row! (I WANT TO KNOW)

Alright, my pet ... Sit up there and I'll tell you, while I'm putting on my face. (*Settling Mister Fluff*). Sit. Goodboyyyy.

At her make-up table ROSE *inspects her face in the mirror.*

Henry was my lover –

Rarohh? (WHAT?)

Before you were born, my peppermint ... 1975, the Irish Stone Age. No PCs, nor mobile phones, nor avocados ... But oh my God, there was Henry. He was gorgeous ... It was the curls you saw first. Black ringlets you could sink your hand into. And his eyes ... I couldn't believe my fortune when I found myself walking down Grafton Street on his arm. More like sailing, it was, than walking. He wore a suit – no tie – and a white shirt open to the throat. Heads turned; I glowed. He pulled me over to a window in BTs (which was on the other side of the street then). 'That blouse in there,' he said, 'it's your colour. Rose for my Rose. Promise me you'll never go out without wearing that colour.'

Raharrr-hmm (GIVE ME A BREAK).

Yeh, it sounds goopy now ... He said it again. 'Promise, promise, say it out loud, Rose ...' And there was this look in his eye, and I could see that he expected me to do as he said, and if I didn't ... 'I promise,' I said, fast enough. 'I do, I do.' Then he whisked me into the shop and bought it – the blouse – just like that, not a sniff at the price tag.

Ruff! (WOW)

Oh yes, I was dazzled. It's like this ... when I was with Henry, I felt confident. Course I wasn't. Why would I be, when I was just up from the country, and hadn't a notion about people, or taking care of myself, or anything at all, beyond knowing that I wanted nothing of the village louts who hung about gawking and passing vulgar remarks ... Yeh, back then, I knew nothing – except how to type ... What I wanted, Mister Fluff, what I really wanted, was a life. And I thought Henry –

During the following, Rose begins to apply her make-up, which continues, as appropriate, throughout the rest of the play.

Anyway. Never underestimate the power of make-up, Mister Fluff. The key lies in the foundation. When your underpinnings are right, the other stuff drops into place. Which, clever as he was, Henry never grasped. What passed for his foundation was quicksand. Yes, Henry was devoid of moral anchor – which unfortunately led to my, eh ... Will I call it my deflowering?

It was madness, climbing over that railing ... Early November. Dark, cold, dry. When I came out of the office where I typed badly, Henry was lying in wait. I was so surprised, I couldn't speak. He stared at me, that scary look, then he pressed his fingers hard on my cheekbones. 'C'mon, Rose,' he said. 'We're going to climb into Merrion Square.'

Back then, the square was locked up tighter than a box. Nobody'd touched it for years ... And there I was, scrambling over the railings into a jungle of overgrowth that was rumoured to be overrun by feral cats. The city vanished in a puff. I could see nothing, only the shadow of him, bulky and dark, as he pulled me along, branches slapping and clawing at me. 'Hurry on,' he said, 'hurry.' I grasped his hand more tightly, afraid to let go. I felt his powerful fingers, the heat of him, his pumping pulse. And we stumbled on into a little clearing, where Henry spread out his coat and pushed me down ...

Rrrrur. (WHIMPER).

(*Silence*).

I must have lost consciousness. It was the pain that brought me round. The burn inside, my throbbing back. I was dazed and cold. Then I heard a voice. Henry's. Disembodied in the night, talking, talking. I picked out a word. *Cathedral.* Cathedral? Was I mad? There was more – strange stuff about building a cathedral in the square. 'But who needs a cathedral when the sky is over our heads? And I'm telling you now, Rose. I'm going to have four children: Grace, Christian, Faith, Benedict.'

The mention of children bumped me back. 'So ... we're going to ... get married?' The question hovered. Henry laughed. 'Next thing,' he said, 'you'll want to go house-hunting.'

Just so, our little relationship began. I wouldn't hear from him for days, then up he'd pop on my doorstep, roses in hand, or a box of chocolates. 'Surprise!' he'd say. 'I like surprises.' Once I caught him eyeing my bedsit with a curling lip. But that's what Dublin was back then, shabby. You wouldn't believe the dirt-encrusted windows, the peeling wallpaper, the smell of coal in the air that you could feel in your throat.

Henry had hijacked my life. I never stopped thinking about him. I pretended he was there when he wasn't, his voice in my ear, his musky scent in my nostrils. And as I lay alone in my bed at night, I imagined his body about to descend on mine, my hands lost in his dark curls. I was in love, Mister Fluff. Though it wasn't quite what I'd imagined love to be ... With Henry, everything was always now, never next week. 'You've bewitched me, Rose,' he'd say, 'body and soul.' I believed him – every word – and never troubled my head with what he didn't say.

The fact is, we saw only bursts and gasps of each other.

Ten days before Christmas, he called for me in his sports car. 'A surprise to end surprises,' he said. What could it be? But he switched on the radio and said no more ... We ended up in Killiney, on the Vico Road. Dublin Bay glittered on our left, stark and wintry. 'Look up,' he said. There were steps, steep steps that led to a house perched on the side of the hill.

Inside, it was unlike anything I'd ever seen ... all sea and light, an enchantment of odd corners and cosy spaces. A world away from my shabby bedsit, from the country town I'd left.

'You like?' Henry said. He peered at my face and laughed. 'Cat got your tongue, so?' he said; and then and there, he set in motion arrangements with the estate agent to buy it, just as casually as if it were a blouse.

Eh-ruf-ruff ... (AMAZING)

He pulled my strings like I was a puppet ... Over the years, I've worked out how he made his pile. It started with gambling and went on from there. What he thrived on, Mister Fluff, was identifying weakness in others, then profiting from it.

Of course I never lived in that castle in the air ... On Friday, he phoned the office, where I typed badly. 'Buy tomorrow's paper,' he said. 'Check out the engagements.' Another surprise. So like him, I thought, as if I knew what he was really like. I hardly slept that night, as my mind danced over the happily-ever-after that beckoned. In the morning, I skipped to the newsagents, high on romance. I turned to the appropriate page, and there indeed was Henry Harring's name ... but the name enshrined beside it? It wasn't mine.

Rrrur. (WHIMPER).

You wouldn't treat an animal like that ... What Henry liked most of all was being brutal.

Applying eye make-up, Mister Fluff, is a delicate task. When it's right, it creates depth and dimension, it brings out the colour of the eyes. When it's wrong, it's cartoonish ... Midnight blue, today: good colour for a funeral ...

Of course, I was shattered. As I relived every moment that we'd spent together, each one emerged in a painful light ... Now, when I passed Merrion Square, I wondered just how many others had leapt over those railings after him, unaware that his sights were settled already on a heifer with a thriving family business behind her. I was never the same again ... But somehow, days passed, then weeks and months ... And there were swings and roundabouts.

One of the solicitors for whom I worked was emigrating, and would I give his doggie a loving home? 'Yes,' I whispered. 'Yes, I will, yes.' Bailey was a bichon frisé, just like you, Mister Fluff, and from the get-go he looked at me exactly like you're looking at me now. The way Henry looked at himself in the mirror.

Harrgh-harrgh-harrgh!

Glad you're laughing, my sweetness ... I always say you can never wear too much blue eye shadow, but you can ... Anyway, life, as it turned out, is a mad, joyous thing. Bailey was my new beginning, my hope, my light, my chance to look out instead of in. When I saw the advertisement for make-up artistry, I was ready.

With make-up, I could change myself. But all the pots and potions and protheses empowered me to change other people too. I can take a plain woman and transform her into a beauty. And I can turn a good-looking man into a monster, which I did with gusto – and with such artistry – that I was picked up by the film industry.

I prospered. I couldn't forget Henry, but he receded from that place in the centre of my heart. He became a sort of ... hobby. I sought him out in the papers, and later, on the internet. His fingers could be found in so many pies. He revelled in his reputation as the bad boy of moneymen, and there were always women – the latest models. But over the years, the photographs grew less and less attractive. His features coarsened. The curls vanished and a hairpiece appeared. He came to have an aura of corruption about him, which I could have helped him with. Had he asked.

Nothing prepared me for the shock of actually seeing him, three weeks ago, and you'd never guess where.

Raur-ruf-ruf!

Exactly. In front of Brown Thomas ... My goodness, how he'd run to fat. Flesh bubbled over his hands and face, and presumably, the unthinkable bits covered by his expensive suit. I stopped him. Yes, I stepped right out in front of that blown-up bully and blocked his path. 'Henry,' I said, 'you look ill. You look miserable. You look like a man who has outlived his time.'

His eyes crawled over me, noting my fitness, my style. He hadn't a clue who I was, and it bothered him ... 'Oh, use your brain, Henry.' I waved my rose-coloured sleeve under his sweaty nose. He stared, uncomfortable as hell. Then recognition began to suck him in like a flooding tide.

'Rose,' I said ... He twitched. He sneered. Then that menacing look came into his eyes, his instinct to intimidate and crush me ...

Don't get mad, I thought, get even.

So I said, 'I'm a witch. Maleficent. Circe. Elphaba. I put a curse on you that has returned with interest all the misery you gave me ...' He stepped backwards, he tottered. For twenty seconds I relished the horror in his eyes. Then I moved aside and let him waddle off ... That was three weeks ago ... I like to think that I frightened him to death.

There. Nearly done. Always save the lippy for last. My signature colour, Romance Rose. Which as it happens, matches exactly the colour of my areolas. And how's about a dab for you, a wisp on the lower lip?

Errrreurrr. (LOVELY)

Mmm, it suits ... And here's the joke, my sweetheart. I never cursed him at all. What did I know about cursing – then? Besides, in a perverse kind of way, wasn't Henry the making of me?

Men! After Henry, I didn't bother. I prefer a 24/7 kind of love. A love that burns brighter every day. After Bailey, there was Baxter. Then Cappuccino. And just at the moment, well ... isn't it yourself, Mister Fluff?

Ruff!

Funny how I'm the one who had the four babies, all by myself ... Looks like we're ready. (*Opening a stylish tote*). Hop in there, my little peppermint.

Ruf-ruf!

Aren't you the picture ... (*She kisses him*). Mwah! Come on, let's you and I go party over the corpse of Henry Harring ... And, should it happen that at a particularly lugubrious point in the service, you feel the urge to scamper up the aisle with a view to sinking your sharp white canines into his fat dead calf ... well, my dear, don't hold back.

Ahuuururrr ... (OH REALLY)

Of course you wouldn't. You're so well-behaved ... But let's imagine it, and relish the joy.

END

Sheila Barrett

ANN AND THE PRINCESS

When Ann was in fifth class, her mother's sister came back
from America for a visit. It was 1960, and Aunt Celia had a
white wool coat and long white boots and a good job in
New York City, and Ann's mother was in a state over her.
'Not that good a job,' Ann heard her tell her father. Waked
up by their voices one night, she had drifted down to the
kitchen for a drink of water. Her mother wasn't angry, she
was crying. 'Anyone will know she can't afford the half of
that! She'll never be able to come back here to live, never.'

'Why wouldn't she?' Ann asked, sleepily. 'Wouldn't you
put her up?'

'Ah, dear, did we wake you? New York, now that's an
exciting sort of place when you're young,' said her father,
who was always the diplomat. 'Your mother misses Celia
is all.'

It's extraordinary what comes back to you when you're
old, Ann thinks, perching on the side of her bed, pulling
on socks, pulling on knickers, tugging on her trousers with

the elasticised waist, and then shoes with the Velcro straps. Careful. Everything careful. Auntie Celia wouldn't have been caught dead in this gear, not if she was a hundred.

Now she's got one foot in Purgatory herself, Ann feels free to talk with the dead. 'Bet you were buried in hot pants,' she tells Auntie Celia, 'or at least you wanted to be. And you' – she turns to Barry's picture on her bedside table – 'you'd better look after this phone!'

Barry, who had taken to digital objects like a duck to water, had died in his sleep in this very bed, taking his expertise with him.

Wrench on the bra, the light wool jumper. Her jacket's downstairs with her coat and her case, all packed for the nursing home. Her handbag's at the foot of the bed, where she asked Martina to leave it. She dumps Barry's picture into it, her phone and its charger. Then she examines her wallet: everything's there.

'Why do you want your passport?' Martina had asked.

'So the Devil will know who I am.'

'Oh, Mum.'

'I don't want to be like those poor Ukrainians handing their identities over to Putin.'

'Heather Haven is hardly Siberia,' said her daughter, her eyes starting to glisten.

'Don't mind me, love. I know it isn't.'

And it's all there: her free travel card, her library card, her driver's licence – what a joke!– and her credit cards – hurray! – and of course the passport. And four twenty-euro notes. 'My Martina's like you,' she tells her dead mother. 'She's sweet, bless her.'

The night before, Martina and Bernard brought dinner from deVille's and put it out on the dining-room table on the best plates, leaving their spouses and children behind.

The three of them talked about all sorts of things, family stories, the houses they'd lived in.

'You never met Auntie Celia, of course,' Ann remarked.

'That might have explained quite a lot,' said her son, but kindly. 'Still got the "running-away money"?'

'I was dying to visit her, but Mam just became apoplectic. We listened to our mothers in those days.'

'But Granny went out herself, didn't she?'

'Only when they were old and he'd died. Even then she wouldn't visit Celia in the apartment. The Palace of Sin, she called it.'

'Riverside Drive, not bad,' said Bernard.

'I'd have made her take me, only I'd just had you.'

'Sorry, Mum.'

'Celia had such good stories. I was so fed up that year she came here – it was *Peig* at school, and she was chatting with me up in my room and I was moaning about *Peig* – 'It's always raining,' and she laughed and said, 'The really cutting morality tales are set in sunshine,' and she told me this – American – fable about an Indian princess.'

'Go on.'

'Oh, you know, Martina – the King of the Prairie brings the princess to his field of corn, and he invites her to step along the row to choose the finest ear to plant, so that she and her people will have corn forever. So she moves along and all the ears are healthy and bursting with life, but she's convinced the next will be better and then ... she's got to the end of the row and she's chosen nothing. And that's what she gets!'

'A bit mean of him,' said Bernard.

Later, foostering in the kitchen – for the last time, for the last time – Ann heard Martina say, 'Is it safe for Mum to have all those cards?'

'Of course not,' said Bernard. 'But sure, what will she order in there besides books?'

'Yeah. Or treats for the kids,' Martina said sadly. 'Should you stop them, though? The cards? In case someone would, you know ...'

Ann, hovering now behind the door, went cold.

'No, Martina. I don't fancy ending my relationship with Mum just yet.'

Ann's shoulders slumped with relief.

'I don't know who he's like,' she tells Barry, peering at his picture as she zips her bag shut. 'He's nicer than either of us.'

She looks at her watch. Thirty-five minutes. It's all right. She'll have a glass of water with her tablets, but no breakfast. She opens her bag again. All her medicine's there in a Ziploc. She opens the curtains. Weak morning light strays into the bedroom. 'So I'm going,' she tells Barry. 'I will never look at that dressing table of your mother's again.' As if in reproach, the heavy mirror sends her image back at her. On the way to grab her comb, she almost falls, whacking her hand against the footboard. 'You eejit.' Deep breath. 'Goodbye, room. We were happy here, as happy as two people like us could be.'

For the first time since his death, she hears Barry talking back to her. 'Two people like us? Mind yourself on those stairs and remember you'll have to pee!'

'I will ... I will!' So he's coming too, her darling. 'Trip of a ... well, not quite a lifetime,' she tells him, negotiating each step, gripping the chill wooden bannisters down to the hall. 'Last time we'll half-freeze our hands on our own bannisters, isn't it, Barry? If you're with me, what else will I need in this old house, or anywhere?'

Her case, packed for the nursing home, waits by the front door with her stick. 'Only the essentials, please, for starters,' she'd told the children, when Martina had protested at the scant wardrobe she'd got out.

Twenty minutes. 'Don't rush.' She walks carefully into the dining room and, heart beating a little faster – 'None of that!' she tells it – she pulls Volume I of Gibbon's *Decline and Fall of the Roman Empire* off the shelf. 'Finally a use for you, you old so-and-so.' Carefully, she removes her travel documents and zips them into her bag.

'Pee,' says Barry. 'Now.'

'Yes, my love.'

When the taxi comes, she's ready.

Martina and Bernard lurk behind the crowds at Departures until they spot their mother, eyes shining, handbag and stick on her lap, being wheeled towards Security.

'Not at the end of the corn row yet, is she?'

'This can't happen.'

'It's her "running-away money". Nothing we can do.'

Martina gathers herself. 'Why did you call me, then, Bernard, when you know I'll stop her? All right, she can keep loving you and be furious with me. Enough is enough.'

'Enough is never enough.'

'Alone?'

'Like we'd have brought her? She knows we can't leave. She's got herself this far. Tell the truth and shame the Devil: would you rather die in front of the TV in Heather Haven or on the top of the Empire State Building in New York City? Look at her now, chatting to that lad pushing her.'

'If that's who she is chatting to.'

They watch as Ann is wheeled past the long queues, as she disappears.

Martina fumbles in her pockets. 'All right. I think I get it. But this is still on you, brother.'

He puts his arm around her, and she jabs him with her elbow. 'I'll hang on here till take-off. In case she changes her mind.'

'Ok.' She shakes her head. 'Jesus, Bernard! Just call me.' She hurries off, wiping her eyes.

The kitchen smells faintly of last night's dinner. The rest of the house smells like itself, but it's a disturbed, 'leaving' smell, Bernard thinks, not the 'greeting' whiff they'd get coming back after a holiday. He opens the curtains in the sitting room and turns off the light.

Volume I of *The Decline and Fall* lies open on the dining-room table. He'd taken it out to borrow when his mother and Martina were together in the kitchen, and it was then he discovered the tickets, the boarding pass and the itinerary. He photographed them and put them back. How many times had his father said, 'You want to go into politics, you'd better read Gibbon.'

'You're very quiet, Bernard,' his mother had said. 'Are you not hungry?'

He smiled, but he couldn't meet her eye. To be honest, it was Martina who could do with a stint in Heather Haven. She and Jack worked at home all through Covid, the twins bottled in with them, supposedly studying. Masked and scrubbed, Martina checked on Ann and cleaned for her. Bernard took over at weekends. If Ann wasn't deteriorating, she was at least changing. She would forget he was there. He supposed it was harmless, her talking to the dead, his father, mostly, and Mrs Lennon from across the road who died in a nursing home during lockdown. And of course, Auntie Celia.

'Do you think about Auntie Celia a lot, Mum?' he'd asked, putting the emptied bin back under the sink.

'I do.'

'Why?'

'Ah, she was never cooped up like this, was she?' She laughed, but then she became serious. 'Who comforted her at the end, Bernard? Who ever visited her grave?'

That day, the entire side of his mother's face was purple from a fall she had. He hoped it would fade a little before Martina saw it.

'Have you ever heard of the New York Stonehenge?' she went on. 'The sun comes from both ends of the streets. Or something. That's when Celia met her man. He said it was a "Sign".'

'Men who talk about "Signs" should have a warning sign.'

She gave him a bright, abstracted smile.

He takes up the book to replace it, and a thin envelope falls out of the back of it. It's stamped and addressed to him and Martina. 'You forgot to post this,' he mutters. 'What else did you forget?'

He checks the locks and slams the front door behind him. In his car, he rips open the envelope.

Dear Martina and Bernard, in clotted biro. *I'm sorry. I'll be good as gold ~~if~~ when I'm back. You know that advert on TV? There's this lizard riding on this little round hoover – for carpets – and he imagines he's in New York having adventures. That's me but ~~I really~~ I want to go in reality. I'll be careful. Then Heather H. will be ~~good~~ perfect. Thank you for finding it. I love you. Thank you for everything. Mum xxxxxxxxxx* With a final blob.

'It's that blob, Mother,' he mutters. 'The blob of unknowing. The blob of ...' His reflection, gaunt and harassed, glares back at him from the windscreen.

A digitally-enhanced lizard, whizzing unscathed through a city street, plummeting down the incline at a skateboard park, mouth open with – joy, or terror? His mother, leaning forward in her chair, laughing. Stories. 'Moving on from corn. A feckin' lizard.'

The sun shines through the windscreen, and he's starving.

Louise C. Callaghan

CASEMENT'S MONUMENT

You'll see a man
dressed for Kingstown,
his back to the sea
and further travel:
Congo, the Amazon
River, Brazil ...
His bronze looks upon
the LexIcon Library,
its serried redbrick
and skyward windows.
Edwardian-bearded,
in a three-piece suit.
A knighted servant
of the Empire,
he turned traitor.
He was executed
after the Easter Rising.
We question him
still, our Irish patriot.
I hear the talk, daily.

HAPPY DAYS

Rocky stage, strange burren
for a Beckett play –

here in the open air.
Not a single tree

to shelter or harbour us
from the blazing sun.

But the elements,
wind, sea, sky, rock

are balanced evenly
around them:

Winnie, with her hold-all
handbag, and Willie,

scraping towards her.
A pair of unhoused birds.

Mary Rose Callaghan

CIAO, CARLA

In my mid-twenties, I taught at a girls' boarding school on the outskirts of Oxford. The city was beautiful and the school down a leafy lane, but it seemed the end of the world to me. I was lonely the way young people are and missed Ireland. Having broken with my boyfriend, I lived a Jane Eyre-like existence. I slept in an attic bedroom and worked non-stop, teaching, marking piles of copy books and even checking end-of-term laundry lists. I taught current affairs to the seniors, and English to most of the lower school, with religion and rounders thrown in. I had wanted to be a writer but it was too difficult. Teaching was a substitute. If I couldn't write books, I could read them. But there was no privacy in the school and the work was endless. I even developed a facial tic.

Carla was the Italian au pair. She was having difficulty with English and always came into the staffroom when I was on duty. I can still see her, bent over an English dictionary and writing in a notebook. 'Maree, what dis mean?'

How to describe her? Think Sophia Loren, or one of those new-age continental film stars. She smelt of cologne and was always beautifully dressed. Her clothes had Dior labels, giving the impression of wealth. So I assumed she was an impoverished aristocrat, that her family had come down in the world. Otherwise, she'd be attending some London language school. When not depressed, she had an Italian gaiety and, despite her beauty, a puppy-like vulnerability. The staff was entirely female, so all the boyfriends and husbands were in love with her. But this didn't make us hate her. On the contrary, we did everything to make her happy, even irritating the school authorities by taking her to a university ball, where rich students in evening dress sprayed champagne at each other. But no matter what we did, Carla was homesick. Unhappiness was a bond between us: I was overworked and she pined for Italy.

I had dissuaded her from returning home several times, but couldn't change her opinion of England's green and pleasant land. In the staffroom one evening, she wrapped herself in her cardigan, shivering. 'I go home.'

'Why sad?' I had to speak her lingo to be understood.

She made a face. 'Reece pudding!'

We'd had rice for dessert that day. 'What's wrong with that?'

'No sugar in reece!' She made to retch. 'And lunch today!'

The food wasn't bad for a school. But that day's treat was a stuffed sheep's heart, so I didn't blame her. Being an animal lover, I had trouble even looking at it. But as a form mistress, I had to finish my plate. The same wasn't true for Carla.

Despite these drawbacks, she agreed to stay till the end of the school year. In return for my friendship, she invited me to visit her family for August. I had only been on the continent once – for a few magic days in Paris – so I was thrilled to be going again. Mid-July came round quickly. Then there was the summer school. I had signed up to teach English as a second language for extra holiday money. My students, more exuberant Italians, went on strike when I put some of them up a class. It was the high point of my career, so I was predisposed to love long-legged Italy.

It was before Ryanair. I landed in sultry Rome airport on a rickety charter from Gatwick. Carla, glamorous as always, was waiting in Arrivals and waved as I came through the barricade. I remember she wore a red headscarf tied pirate-like around her head, a blue check shirt and tight jeans. She carried a big designer shoulder bag and, after we embraced, said there was a change of plan: we weren't going south to her home, but north to a French resort, near Beaulieu. We were staying in a hotel with her boyfriend Carlo's extended family, who vacationed there yearly.

I must've looked worried, because she offered to pay.

'Oh, no!' I said. 'I am rich now.'

Carla was expecting Carlo for a week. Their matching names had always struck me as comic. I had heard everything about the affair: the ups and downs, the ons and offs. How he was a rich lawyer who owned Picasso paintings and other valuables. How she wanted to marry him, but he wouldn't oblige.

I dragged my case after her to the airport taxi rank. In the cab, she pointed to a photograph of an Oxford college in a guide book. 'You say ... I study here – in Magdalene College. I in university, not bad school.'

I hesitated. 'OK ... but we're not bad school.'

She looked unconvinced. 'You say I at Oxford University?'

I sighed. 'How did we meet?'

'You my professor?'

'*What?*'

She passed the guide book. 'Look, Magdalene? I go there.'

'It's pronounced *Maudlin,* by the way.'

This puzzled her. 'How ees that?'

'English isn't always pronounced how it's spelt.'

I wasn't sure which college was which but knew Magdalene was near the bridge. On one occasion, I had taken summer-school students on a guided tour of the university and got lost, so I invented the names of the colleges. No one had noticed. But Roman aristocrats would be different. If you're lying, it's best to get the details right. As well as being a professor, I found myself promising to pretend Carla was dating a young member of the House of Lords – they had met at the university. Would anyone believe this fantasy?

She pocketed the book, pouting. 'I naver learn.'

'Never say never.'

'Naver say naver,' she repeated, shouldering through crowds to the station.

We caught the train north and shared our carriage with an Italian family. I remember their happiness and generous offers of bread and salami. I was in Italia, where the people were generous, children were loved, and the wine flowed. But would France be as good? And what would it be like staying in a hotel with a big family without knowing their language? I was experiencing what Carla had suffered in England.

Beaulieu is over the border from Monte Carlo. The Riviera turned out to be another world. The sea, the sun, the sand, the rich villas terracing Mediterranean hills. Cafés with tables on the street served croissants and coffee. The hotel was out of town and almost on a beach. The well-bred aura of my hosts, who seemed to have rented the entire place, mesmerised me. I had never met people like this and imagined myself a character in the film *Death in Venice*. By day, the family sat under big umbrellas on the manicured sand, either oiling themselves or going for swims. There was a siesta in the afternoon and aperitifs were served as they gathered for a late dinner. Then grandparents, uncles, aunts, parents, children and grandchildren sat down to dinner at a long table and worked through several courses: antipasti, pasta, a main course, cheese, desert and fruit. All with appropriate wines. There was laughter and chat, which I didn't understand. The women were beautiful and the men distinguished. My clothes weren't up to theirs. I fancied myself above fashion, but on arrival Carla had brought me to an expensive boutique, which sold *de rigueur* bikinis. So I too could sit half-naked under umbrellas.

Carlo finally arrived. I remember him as handsome in an Italian way, but oily with a macho sneer. When Carla introduced us in the beach bar, he was wearing city clothes: black patent shoes, a white open-necked shirt tapering into narrow trousers. He looked my bikini up and down in approval or disapproval, I'm not sure which, and offered me a drink. I didn't imbibe much then, so ordered espresso. While Carla and he chatted in Italian, I pretended to understand.

I slept in a child's cubicle, next to their ensuite bedroom. My bed was narrow as a nun's, and sounds of nightly love-making kept me awake. I thought of the boyfriend who had dumped me. Would I ever find love? Now and again, there were loud noises, but I put this down to continental exuberance. This was the Riviera after all. Some of the world's most passionate operas were set here. Love was in the air.

Carla was busy with Carlo most of the time. I read my book and studied Italian. I got the bus into Nice one day and Monte Carlo another. I visited a Matisse gallery and Princess Grace's kingdom, lighting a candle in her cathedral. On other days, while everyone else had an afternoon siesta, I walked the beach – to the end and then back again, seeing only fishermen who waved at me. It wore me out, so I slept better. The Mediterranean was cobalt blue, a little darker than the sky. The sun shone every day. A person could do anything here, I thought. The happiness was infectious. At one endless dinner I found myself sitting next to Carlo's uncle, a professor in a Roman university. I don't remember what he was a professor of, or if I ever knew. I suppose he was about sixty-five which was ancient to me then. We spoke in my bad French and then broken English.

'I hear you professor, Maree?' he said.

I cleared my throat. What was he saying? Then I remembered my promise to Carla.

'You teach Eengleesh, yes?'

'Yes! Eh, that's right. Eh, literature.'

It was true in a way. He wouldn't be able to check. Oxford was too far away.

He frowned. 'You like sherry?'

I held up my glass. 'No, eh – I'm a wine person.'

'Sherry eeze grate poet, no?' He looked sad. 'He come to Italia. He drown in sea.'

'Oh ... you mean Shelley!'

'You like?'

'I prefer Keats. He died in Rome.'

He shook his head sadly and the conversation ended. I wasn't forced to tell any more lies. The professor had a boat, a rib, and promised to bring me out in it before I left. He wagged a warning finger. 'You swim correctly?'

I assured him I did. My childhood had been spent swimming, and I had a passable dog paddle. I disliked being out of my depth, but felt I'd be safe with an experienced boatman. On the last day of the holiday, he kept his promise and brought me out in his rib. We dropped anchor a distance from shore and I swam around the boat. The water was a cold and deep, but I wasn't afraid, it was blissful really. The professor lay in the boat, reading a book under a straw hat, and we returned after about an hour. But coming in to shore, a huge wave caught us. The boat overturned and I was thrown out, along with the professor. I remember the scrape of stones on the beach and the swish of water as the wave receded. But I only got a few scrapes. The professor must have been shocked, but ran to my aid. 'You have brandy, yes?'

I had two and got a fit of the giggles. I couldn't stop laughing, which must have been shock. Our lucky escape was the topic of conversation at dinner. The family gesticulated wildly. What if the engine propellers had cut off our arms or legs?

It was my last night in the lonely little room. As usual I fell asleep to the sounds of passion, but awoke sometime later to Carla's scream. Then loud slapping and Carlo shouting in Italian. What was he doing to her? At first, I lay there listening. There was silence, then more shouting and hitting. I got my courage up and knocked on their bedroom door.

Carla opened it, looking tousled and teary.

'You OK, Carla?'

She looked at the ground.

'I heard ...'

'Me fine, Maree.'

'Are you sure?'

'Yes. You sleep now.'

'Ok ... night then.'

There was no more shouting, but Carla wasn't at breakfast the next morning. I had my croissant and coffee alone, then went for my last walk on the beach. Carla and I caught a train back to Rome and then a bus to the southern city where her family lived. She never referred to the previous night.

As the bus droned along the highway, I broke the silence. 'I was worried last night, Carla.'

She looked puzzled. 'Why?'

'Carlo ... ?'

She sighed wearily. 'He try force me.'

'He can't do that!'

She looked out the window. 'He no like tame love.'

I didn't know what to say. Was this usual in Italy? Was it all rubbish about it being the country of love? I don't know if it was worry about Carla or a week of semi-monastic silence but I started crying. What was wrong with me?

She put an arm around me. 'You find nice man one day, Maree. Man like Carlo.'

I didn't know what to say. Things aren't always what they seem. But Carla's parents made up for Carlo's bad behaviour. They were happy Italians who lived an ordinary life in a high-rise apartment. I had a wonderful three weeks, meeting the grandmother and the younger brother, eating delicious pasta and fresh fish, discovering pizza, sunbathing on a beach. There was a wonderful art gallery in the city and Carla's parents brought me on a trip to Perugia. I didn't learn much Italian but understood most conversations by the end of the month. It's always been my dream to go back to Italy. I've been back for a few short holidays, but not long enough to learn the language.

Carla didn't want to return to the school and offered to get me a job teaching in a Roman Berlitz. We would both live in the eternal city.

'You meet nice man, Maree. Buy nice clothes.'

I was tempted but couldn't make a decision. The school was difficult but it was a job. I had worked hard to get a degree.

'Stay,' Carla said.

I shook my head. Was I making a mistake?

'Onore,' she sighed.

Carla came back with me to Oxford but left after a few weeks. I got pneumonia in the middle of the Easter term and returned to Ireland. I wrote to Carla a few times, but she never replied. I know you can't live every life, but I missed her and Italy. It was my road less travelled.

Susan Connolly

THE SEA

WHEN THE SEA THUNDERS ACROSS
HIGH SANDBANKS AND FLOODS
YOU WITH ITS SOUND I HEAR
ITS SOLEMN ROAR 100 MIL-
ES AWAY. WHEN DAY IS
BRIGHT-CLEAR AND
YOU CAN SEE FOR
MILES CAN YOU
SEE MORE
DEEPLY
INTO
ME
?

```
from  the  blue - grey  laneway
                    i
                  see  a
                  stripey
                  estuary
the  boyne                        b
      c                           i
    c   u                         r
    u   r                         d
    r   l                         s
      v   i                    on  the
        i   n                  mudflats
          n  g                      e
            g                         e
                                        d
                                          i
                                            n
                                              g
s
m                    i
ell  of  sand              curlews
                    t            r
                    h        y  louder  at
                    h
                    e  air                    d
                                              u
                                              s
                                              k


                    i
                  stand
                  beside
                my  bike
                    t
                    h
                  n   i
                    o  n
                    t  k
                      h  i
                        i  n
                          n  g
                            g
```

```
w a k i n g   e a r l y


w
a
k
i n   e a r l y   m o r n i n g
n             i
g             g
              h
              t
      a
        w i d e
          a
          k
            e
      i
            a
            l i e
            o
            i n   s i l e n c e
            e
                          s
                        d
                      r
                    o
            n o   w
            n o t     a   s o u n d
            n o   m
                  u
                    s
                      i
                        c
      i
                  l
                n   i
                e   s
                  t
          t o   m y
        t h o u g h t s
      t
      h
i n   e   e a r l y   m o r n i n g
```

Colette Connor

On the Road with Fellini

Whenever I pass there,
I think of you in your wheelchair,
Waving your stick and shouting:
'This is like a Fellini movie!'

So it was: there in the sunlight,
Two sisters making their way
Across the road knowing
One was facing death.

That day it was all lightness;
The scream of fate forgotten
As we laughed in the sunshine,
Happy in each other's company.

At least you left me that;
That last memory of you at your best,
Before your life faded out to show
A woman who, like Fellini,

Looked life full in the eye
Without ever showing how expert
She was at cutting out
Sentiment and tenderness.

ALICE SPRING

She admits to a sick stomach and, already,
There is evidence of death in her face;
Her eyes have lost the will to live,
She exists on borrowed days.

Yet, beneath it, the young girl remains;
The one who looks with sympathy at the world,
Who gives every spare penny to charity;
Despite her own impoverishment and neglect.

Since old God's time she had lived between floors,
And who knows what crucifixions
Take place behind the anonymity of walls,
The shattered lives lived out behind closed doors.

Suffered lives unseen and unheard,
Lives lived to the beat of a distant clock,
To the advent of sunrise and sunset,
And the unworn clothes left hanging in wardrobes.

Catherine Dunne

The Light of Home (*extract*)

2023

Rachael pushes the door open and steps across the threshold. A spiderweb, fine and silvery, launches itself at her face. She tries to bat it away, but it clings to her lips, insistent. The shadowy, earthy smell of mushrooms catches the back of her throat. She stands still for a moment, waits for her eyes to adjust to the grainy interior.

She looks down the long hallway, sees its tiles faded and cracked. Someone has ripped the copper piping out of the internal wall. The plaster gapes; she hears the rustle of something within as it scuttles its way down to the skirting board. Quickly, she moves away and steps through the opening where an oak door used to be. She makes sure to watch where she places her feet.

The floor is littered with fragments of sea-coloured glass; shattered photograph frames, their contents long gone; a single shoe. She recognises the small table that staggers drunkenly in one corner. Old newspapers peer from under cracked linoleum. And then there's the dust: the swirling motes above her, around her, lying thickly on every exposed surface.

The large room feels like some kind of underworld after the brittle light outside. She stands at its centre, waits for her crooked heartbeat to become right again. The restless ghosts around her begin to take shape and her children's names fling themselves at her, randomly, out of air that is slowly becoming light. Síle, Iarlaith, Aoife, Brendan, their faces luminous, impossibly young. Young and beautiful, loved. It had never been a question of love: of loving or not loving enough.

Rachael hesitates now, poised halfway between flight and stillness. Finally, she decides and walks quickly towards the French doors that lead to the garden. She feels along the top of the door frame, left to right. Her fingers find what she's looking for. She puts the rusty key into the lock. It grates a little at first, but then gives way. She pushes open the doors and steps out onto the weed-choked patio.

All at once, the garden comes alive with childish voices. Síle, trying to organise Aoife and Iarlaith into playing some complicated game, one where she keeps changing the rules to suit her.

But Aoife is well able to stand her ground. She is a sturdy five-year-old, her fair hair in a fat, warm plait that almost reaches her waist. She clutches her doll to her chest, unwilling to bend to her big sister's demands.

I don't want to, she says. You're not the boss of me.

But you need your two hands to play the game, otherwise it won't work! Síle is aggrieved.

Aoife shakes her head. I don't want to play that game. It's stupid. And she turns on her heel.

Don't call me stupid! Síle wails, but Aoife's not for turning. She marches up the garden towards the house, chin lifted, defiance in every step.

Iarlaith ignores both of them, setting out bits of bread and fat on the bird tables Darragh has made for him. Edith complained once that all those tasty titbits would attract squirrels, mice, and worse. Conor told her to leave the child alone. Rachael overheard him on that occasion, without meaning to. His voice had acquired a hard edge, something that surprised her. Maybe it had started by then, after all: the rot that slowly crept its way through everything that bound them together.

In those days, Conor and Iarlaith shared a strong connection, one forged out of love for the land and all that grew there. They spent hours together, feeding the hens, tending the hedgerows once the nesting season was over, fishing the river that bordered the western boundary of the endless fields.

Rachael can see Brendan as he was then, seated under the plum tree, nose in a book. He often seemed not to belong to his tribe. He alone refused to call her Rachael. He stuck stubbornly to Mum, or if he was out of sorts, Mother. A dreamy child, whose real life – his imaginative life – was lived elsewhere. Off exploring caves, climbing mountains, or adventuring somewhere on the high seas.

She steps carefully through the garden now, past the plum tree, towards the high wall at the end. The shadows of espalier pear trees are smoky against the red brick. The ribs of the old tree house are visible, too, poking their way through the wilderness. But the architecture of the garden is still here: the same structure that emerged the first time they'd hewn a new shape together out of all that wildness. There had been dogwood then, too, and lilac and honeysuckle. A cloudy pink mass of hydrangea still spills its way out from the back wall; abelia and St John's Wort riot their way towards the patio.

She'd loved watching the way the garden had evolved under her fingers, the same way she loved watching form emerge from clay. That exhilarating moment when what she handled ceased to be raw material and became, instead, something infused with the spark of life. It never lost its power to thrill, to claim her. It made everything else fade into a foggy distance so that she ceased to hear, to see, to feel anything but the way her hands moved under their own guidance.

The red-crowned crane was the first piece she'd sculpted for their new garden. It is here still, its faded scarlet head just visible above the weeds. She'd placed it directly under the willows. Willow for resilience, she said.

Darragh had looked at her, his whole face a question. And a crane for fidelity, he replied. She reached out to him then, grasping his hand in hers, feeling the kind roughness of its palm.

That was before Síle. Before all of them.

Brendan

It was those pictures of the caves that did it: that book of wild, almost childish drawings that my father gave me for my sixth birthday. I can see the outline of the bison, the ochre colour of the flesh. I remember almost hearing the rapid beating of the heart beneath all that powerful muscle. It fascinated me. The animal's dignity, its stilled strength, all that rage trapped forever on the walls of a Spanish cave.

That book went everywhere with me. Out into the fields behind the barn, up into the apple trees of Grandpa's orchard, even into the tree house that Dad had made in the sturdy branches of the oak that stood at the end of our garden. I leafed through those pages until the book fell apart.

Then I was inconsolable.

It's ok, son. Dad ruffled my hair in the absent-minded way he had developed by then. I'll get you another one.

He was kindness itself, but he often wasn't present behind his eyes in the days after she left. Days that became months that became years.

He did get me another book: but it wasn't the same as the one that was gone. Its difference made me angry. I wanted the one that was mine: the one with pictures of beasts and tombs and circular houses. Of spears and weapons and scattered cow bones punctured to make ancient whistles. I didn't want something reeking of newness.

Síle and I bickered endlessly over it. As the eldest, she slipped into *her* place, once she was gone.

Can't you just be grateful? she hissed. Why do you always have to upset him?

Even then, at seven, I knew I wasn't what upset him – at least, not completely. There were other things that had happened, huge things that had nothing to do with me.

I used to watch him hovering around that red crane at the bottom of the garden, a piece of her sculpture that I learned to hate. He'd look as if he was going to get busy pruning or digging or collecting plums or whatever: depending on the season.

But mostly, he'd just mope.

A witch, Charlotte had called Rachael on her wedding day.

How else could you've managed all this sunshine in the Irish midlands? she said. It's early May. It's supposed to be raining.

Even the forbidding stone of the big house had lost some of its grey. It looked benign in the sunlight that day, its edges softened by the lines of mountain ash that Conor had planted more than fifty years earlier. *Caorthann*, he called them. He refused to call them ash or rowan; he used only Irish names for all that he grew.

I'm my own planter, he used to say, growing another kind of history.

Early that morning, trestle tables were carried out from the barn and set up in dappled sunlight. At first, Edith had been unwilling.

Your wedding reception, here? She had looked from Darragh to Rachael and back again, her green eyes startled.

It was the first time Rachael had ever seen her so unguarded.

Yes, Darragh said.

Yes, please, Rachael said, nudging him with her elbow.

He grinned. Yes, please, Mother. It's what we want. What we both want, he added. Rachael knew that his mother regarded her as the driving force; she'd said so, and not only once. And perhaps she wasn't wrong.

Ok, then, Conor said, glancing at his wife. I think that's a fine idea. It's time we warmed the bones of this old house, Edith. Get some young blood flowing in its veins again.

Edith didn't look convinced. Rachael had overheard her complain to her husband that she, Rachael, was a hippy. Someone flighty and dreamy and not at all suitable for their youngest son.

Conor had laughed. I believe they call it being a free spirit, my dear. And Darragh is well able to look after himself. He's nearly forty – let him go.

For their wedding, Rachael chose the filmiest, floatiest maxi dress she could find. She wove wildflowers into her long hair, carried a bunch of purple marshlocks tied with a simple ribbon. There were hundreds of guests: Darragh's parents' guests. But that day, she didn't care, didn't feel any of the lingering shadows of absence. The sun shone long into the evening. By the time people started to drift away, heading for home, even Edith looked pleased.

I can't believe my luck, Darragh whispered to Rachael, over and over again. Can't believe you're mine.

1967

Sometimes, I wondered if it was the house I'd fallen in love with rather than Darragh. Something in me responded to the solidity of grey stone, the symmetry of tall windows. I was drawn to the sense of roots planted deep in familiar soil. Everything about it spoke of belonging, of never needing to explain. Its place in the landscape was assured – the house, the outbuildings, the barn – as though they had all grown there, as though the land could never have looked any other way. And there was the affluence, too: in those days it seemed to me to be effortless, unchanging.

I wanted it to be my past, as well as theirs. I wanted it instead of the cramped, shouty, two-up, two-down that I was still trying to leave behind. Darragh was exactly twice my age when we met: his sober thirty-six to my wild-child eighteen.

Over the thumping soundtrack, Mick Jagger in full voice, Charlotte introduced us.

And this is Rachael, she shouted.

I saw her lips move, saw her gesture in my direction, although none of us could hear anything apart from the Stones not getting no satisfaction in that party room.

He offered me a cigarette and while I was still thinking about it, he put his hand under my elbow, warm, firm, steering me towards the hall and the open front door. We sat on the steps together. Cool air, dark sky, stars high and chilly.

I'm Darragh, he said.

I nodded. Hi.

And you're Rachael. He struck a match, cupped one hand around the flame.

I bent towards it, pulling back my hair. Casually. I'd only begun smoking, hadn't really got the hang of it yet. Rachael with two *a*'s, I said.

I'll remember that.

Even then, I could see how eager he was. Earnest, trustworthy. Old, to my eyes.

I looked at him properly as I drew the smoke into my lungs. This time, I managed not to cough. He looked back at me, without blinking.

What has you here? I asked.

Then I was mortified. I'd been aiming for cool. What came out sounded rude. That's your problem, my mother used to say. Everything that goes through your head doesn't have to come out your mouth, you know. You hurt people.

He laughed – a real laugh. Loud, delighted. You mean, what's an old man like me doing at a piss-up like this?

I'd had enough time to gather myself.

No. It's just that I haven't seen you here before. And Charlotte and I know all of each other's friends.

I'm a distant cousin, he said. I've been working in London for years. Just back in the last couple of weeks.

I was surprised. Why would anyone want to come back from swinging London to boring old Ireland?

I can't wait to get away, I said, sounding braver than I felt. This city is dead. Nothing ever happens here.

I'm not really a city person. He sounded thoughtful. I found that out in London. I'm just passing through.

To where?

To my home place.

His withholding intrigued me. I wasn't used to it.

And where is home? I could hear my mother's voice in my ear again. Stop asking so many questions. It's not your place. Mind your manners.

He smiled over at me then. Somewhere way too quiet for you, I think. He stubbed out his cigarette on the stone step and immediately lit another. I watched the tiny sparks fly up into the velvety air, a small explosion of light.

And what about you? he asked. Are you at uni with Charlotte?

Yeah. But I don't know if I'll stick it. I want to go travelling.

Let me guess, he said. To San Francisco, to wear flowers in your hair? He was smiling.

I felt stung. But I didn't show it. Why not? I shrugged. There's nothing for me here.

That was the first time.

Now Rachael sees that the wooden gate on the eastern side of the garden has collapsed in on itself. Its blue paint is flaking and she can count the passage of years by the traces of yellow and green gloss visible underneath. Its appearance pleases her: a shabby-chic palette of shades, telling its own story. She lifts the gate to open it more fully, hears it scrape against the concrete path. She squeezes through the narrow space and makes her way towards the barn. To her surprise, it looks intact. The sun is glinting off the upper windows, the sliding door is partly open.

This isn't right, an internal voice tells her. This barn is long gone, consumed by fire. It shouldn't be here, shining in the sunlight. Rachael's mouth goes dry as she hears a voice, voices, from within. She is about to turn away. This is not why she's come. She doesn't want to make small talk, to explain, to be polite.

But she's not quick enough. The broad door slides open more fully and a woman steps out. She's young, maybe as young as Rachael was when she first came here. She's startled, stares at Rachael's face. Then, as if she's trying to solve a puzzle, looks her up and down with no trace of embarrassment.

Rachael is rooted to the spot. They look at each other, the young and the old, each gaze filled with incomprehension, but neither of them speaks. All Rachael can focus on is the other woman's tumble of auburn hair, eyes of shocking blue.

Finally, the woman wipes her hands on the sides of her jeans. Still, she doesn't take her eyes off Rachael.

'Who are you?' she says at last.

Philomena Feighan

LONG SLEEPS THE SUMMER IN THE SEED *(extract)*

Dublin, 1967. Finn Prendergast, a tutor at UCD, has fallen headlong in love with Marianne Wrixon, a first-year student. Although she is notorious for her wild lifestyle, she chooses Finn because he is attractive without being conceited, caring without being controlling, and – as a tutor – estimable without being conformist. She has been sent over from England to stay with her grandparents while her parents are stationed with the BBC in Iran. Finn suspects that she got pregnant by him to punish her parents for abandoning her in parochial Dublin. Her grandparents, anxious to avoid a scandal in their neighbourhood, offer to pay for an apartment in the city until the birth, after which the baby will be placed for adoption. Marianne's pregnancy is an easy one, but traumatised by the birth, she shuns her baby. Meanwhile, Finn gives tutorials during the day, works at the Anna Livia pub at night, and struggles to find the time to complete his master's thesis.

The arrival of the baby turned Finn's life upside down. Now, instead of working at the Anna Livia at night, he walked up and down the apartment with his son, who contorted and shrieked the progress of colic through his tiny bowels, while Marianne recovered in bed on the other side of a closed door. His teaching job over for the summer, he took daytime work at the pub, knowing that he was mortgaging his academic future by not working on his master's thesis. When he approached Maurice Phelan for an extension on his deadline, he made no mention of his circumstances – other than to cite personal reasons – for fear they would weaken his case. As he expected, Phelan gave him the extra time, but Finn still didn't know when or how he was going to be able to hand the thesis in, even by the extended date.

Nevertheless, his new work schedule meant he could feed and change the baby first thing and settle him back to sleep before opening time at ten-thirty, then get home for an hour once the lunchtime trade had eased, to look after him again. By then Marianne would be waking up. She had nothing to say anymore; the injuries of childbirth had rendered her mute and hostile. They exchanged brief, desultory words on topics like rent and groceries. Other than that, there was silence, broken only by the BBC on the radio. Day after day, she listened to accounts of the Summer of Love in San Francisco and the thousands of hippies flocking to a place called Haight-Ashbury to turn on, tune in, drop out. That's where she belonged, she said on one of the few occasions she could rouse herself to speak. At a be-in, with people like her. Not stuck in a Dublin flat with her cunt held together like a laced shoe.

Her only foray outside the flat was down to Tara Records on Tara Street for Scott McKenzie's single 'San Francisco', playing it over and over to drown out the strident cries of the baby. She also came home with some pills in a brown paper bag, purchased from her former supplier. Finally, she could knock herself out, she said, and take the edge off the pain. One afternoon, when Finn came home for the baby's next feed, he heard his son's shrieks coming down the stairwell. Bolting up to the third floor, he found the baby out in the landing, writhing inside Marianne's suitcase, and pulled him out just as he was about to go into convulsions.

'He didn't disturb anyone,' Marianne said when Finn shook her into consciousness. 'Everyone in the building is off at work.'

Finn comforted himself with the thought that at least she'd left the suitcase open. Still holding the infant, he called a fellow worker from the payphone downstairs to take his shift at the pub. He knew instinctively that he needed to keep the baby close to him to restore its sense of security. His own, too. So he spent the afternoon reading on the sofa, while the baby slept on his chest and Marianne lapsed back into her stupor.

But the more he tried to coordinate his life, the more it disintegrated around him, as if he'd been tasked with making a pyramid of marbles. The daytime work at the Anna Livia meant a smaller clientele, a lower wage and fewer tips. Before long, he realised that he could no longer afford the baby formula, tins of SMA stacked on the pharmacy shelf like a slick, impenetrable wall. Finally out of options, he wrote home to his parents, driven by want like the Prodigal Son to confess his sins and beg for help, all the time imagining the consternation his letter would cause in Drumcalla. But he cared less about that than about no money coming back, so he framed the letter carefully: he loved the girl, and he wanted to do right by her and the baby. Please God, they would be married soon. In the meantime, he continued, he would have to forsake his studies and get a full-time job. He knew the impact such an announcement would have on his mother, the relinquishing of her last hope; and he loathed himself for his premeditation. For his lies, too. Because with each passing day, the prospect of a life with Marianne grew fainter. When he placed an arm around her in bed at night, she shuddered and pushed him away. If he loathed himself, she seemed to loathe him more.

A postal order arrived the following week, enough to keep the baby in formula for months, and Finn thanked his parents in his heart, knowing how many dozen eggs had to be sold to make the payment. He was ready for the anger and the blame, but no letter accompanied the postal order. His mess, the silence connoted. His to figure out.

Marianne had an unequivocal answer, however. As her scars healed and her voice returned, she began to raise the question of adoption. They needed to get rid of it, she said. They'd been living in a cloud.

'Get rid of it,' Finn repeated. 'He's not some insect that got trapped in the flat.'

She nodded in acknowledgement. 'Fair enough. But I promised my grandparents I'd place the baby for adoption. That's why they offered the financial support.'

'Now you're concerned with honouring the bargain you made with them,' Finn said bitterly. 'Before, you mocked them for being so middle class.'

'I'm nineteen, with a baby,' she said. 'How middle class is that?'

'We knew the risks,' Finn said. 'We're talking about our son here. We can't toss him aside, just because you changed your mind.'

'Easy for you to say. You're a man. You can walk away whenever you like.'

'Do you see me walking away?'

Her lip curled. 'Oh, how very noble of you.'

He didn't feel noble. His desire to keep the baby issued from the pit of him, a primal imperative to protect his offspring. Before long, the arguments increased, demolishing their former life together. He was certain he'd come home one day to discover that she'd taken the baby and left him on the doorstep of the Sisters of Charity in Donnybrook.

In the end, it was Marianne who disappeared. On a warm bank-holiday weekend, she bathed, put on a mini skirt and a floral blouse, and went out. When there was no sign of her the following morning, the wild thought occurred to Finn that she had taken off to San Francisco, but he was able to persuade himself to have some sense. He left the baby in the care of his neighbours across the landing, two young secretaries who agreed to leave the doors of both flats standing open so that they might hear the baby if he should cry. Then Finn went in search of Marianne in all her regular haunts. He began with the cafés, the New Amsterdam on South Anne Street and the Bailey on Duke Street, where he drew a blank, but then at the Yeoman on South King Street, a waitress remembered Marianne stopping by the previous day. No, Marianne didn't stay, just long enough to do some business with some of the 'regulars' who operated from a table in the back corner.

That evening, Finn brought the baby across to his neighbours, with two miniature Smirnoff's as payment, and started off on his own odyssey of the pubs that Marianne used to frequent, certain that in her current state of disassociation she would do harm to herself. Able to recognise her by her long blonde hair – and a swarm of men around her – he didn't need to do much more than stand at the door and look around. No sign of her. On then to the clubs: the Moulin Rouge and the Flamingo, where the men at the door knew him and let him in with a nod. He battled his way through the smoke and a crush of bodies dancing to music that reverberated in his fillings. Still no sign.

Then at Club a Go-Go, he got a lead: Marianne was in Skerries for the weekend, raving it up. Finn knew about Skerries, where people went on drug-fuelled rampages that lasted for days. On his way home, he talked himself through a plan of action, although it wasn't much of a plan because it was based on her actions, with him attending upon the outcome. If she got through the weekend without harm, he thought, she'd be home by Sunday evening at the latest. He sat at the kitchen table all Sunday afternoon, waiting for the door to open. Then when the baby settled for the night, he went downstairs to the return and sat facing the front door.

Suddenly the payphone jangled. He tumbled down to the hall to answer it before she hung up, roared into the receiver. 'Hello? Hello?' It was Marianne's grandfather, speaking in cool, measured tones, to say that she was with them. He revealed, only after Finn insisted on knowing, that she'd been dropped off at their house the night before, that Marianne was very much the worse for wear, but that she would soon recover. So not lying dead in someone's bathroom, after all. Finn swallowed hard to control the heaving. But then the grandfather said that he would come by in a few days to pick up her belongings, and Finn knew it was all over. She had gone back to her old beat again, clearly done with him and the qualities that led her to him in the first place. The dam burst in his heart, rising to blind him as he tried again and again to hang up the receiver. He stumbled upstairs like a drunkard. His stomach flipped. He made just in time to the bathroom before vomiting.

Marianne's grandfather arrived at the flat a couple of days later, as the baby was waking up. Once a man of some bearing, he was now bowed, with a lock of silver hair drooping over his forehead, and cheekbones that jutted from a hollowed-out face. He inhaled sharply when he heard whimpering and brushed past Finn into the bedroom, where the baby was stretching in his nest in the bottom drawer of the tallboy.

'So she didn't give the child up for adoption, after all? She told us she had.'

Finn placed himself in front of the tallboy, thinking he'd be able to take the old man down if he tried to snatch the baby.

'I wouldn't have let her in any case,' he said. 'He's my son, too.' He put the pacifier in the baby's mouth to keep him from crying. Buy himself some time.

'But how will you raise him on your own?' the grandfather said. 'It takes two, even in the best of situations. And marriage to Marianne certainly doesn't appear to be a possibility. Nor, to be honest, would I recommend it.'

Finn remembered Marianne's words on their very first morning together: she would never play little missus. It had been a warning from her, but he had been too besotted to listen.

'What happens next, then?' he said.

'I'm afraid my wife and I don't know what to do with Marianne, any more than you do,' the grandfather replied. 'We're at our wits' end. We will send her over to her parents in Teheran. We're too old for this.'

Finn nodded. Marianne liked to spin the illusion of being sophisticated and independent. But she wasn't independent; she did nothing without establishing a safety net first. And there was nothing sophisticated, either, about her instincts for self-preservation which bordered on a reflex, creating destruction for those who took care of her.

The grandfather sighed and reached into his jacket, pulling out his wallet. 'A handsel for the baby,' he said, pushing some large bills into Finn's hand. He would also pay the rent up to the end of the year's lease; after that, Finn was on his own.

The grandfather accepted Finn's offer to help carry Marianne's things. Just as they were leaving the flat, the baby's fretfulness amplified to a howl. Finn stalled. The grandfather looked at him inquiringly. Finn went back inside; he was never going to leave that child crying alone again. Taking a small tablecloth, he tied it around his neck and under his arm like a sling, before picking up his son and placing him against his chest. Then he led the way downstairs, out to the street, record player in one hand, Marianne's LP collection in the other. He stood while the grandfather fumbled with the keys, before loading her belongings into the car, his last material connection to her.

The grandfather smacked down the trunk lid and went around to the driver's side. Before unlocking the door, he turned back to Finn, standing on the sidewalk like a marsupial, the baby wriggling inside the sling.

'What a strange fellow you are,' the old man said.

With all traces of Marianne gone, the flat changed, as if she had placed it under an enchantment. Monastic and silent now, except for the baby's crying, which gave expression to the stupefying loss that strangled Finn's own voice. His duty to feed and burp and change his son was all that got him out of bed in the morning. The money from his parents and the baby's great-grandfather began to dwindle. Soon he'd have to start thinking about finding a job. But he had a long-term duty to his son that stretched beyond part-time pub work, which was lost to him anyway, since he hadn't shown up there in weeks. He needed to secure a proper teaching position at the college. And all that lay in the way was his thesis.

The fog in his head began to clear, giving rise to a sense of purpose. He reached for his bag and pulled out his notes, along with a pad and a pen. Fuck it, how hard could it be, when there were mouths to feed.

That week, and the week following, Finn wrote as if he were draining the running sore of his loss on to the pages of his pad. One page became two, became three. Ever conscious that the baby could awaken at any time, he wrote urgently and without thinking, dashing down phrases, sentences, paragraphs, because everything halted on the mewling of the infant. He stopped one hundred and twenty pages later, first draft done, went out to Hodges Figgis in Dawson Street for some more pads. He bought a naggin of whiskey on the way home, where he toasted himself all evening until the flat began to pitch and toss under his feet. When he sobered up next day, he began the revision, all fear gone now, because he had conquered the blank page.

Another week went by, and then another. The work was good, better than he'd considered himself capable of. He pressed on, hour after hour, while the baby snoozed contentedly in the sling against his chest. When he was finished, he crossed the landing again to his neighbours the secretaries, one of whom agreed to type up his manuscript. This time, he paid her with cash.

Finally, he arrived at the history department in Earlsfort Terrace and stood in front of his advisor. Late, yes, but worth the wait, Finn said. Take it or leave it; he had enough to contend with. Maurice Phelan looked at the baby wriggling in the sling, as if it were a ferret that might suddenly jump out at him, and silently stretched out his hand for Finn's thesis.

Finn couldn't know that Phelan would later award his master's degree ex post facto, and the Stephen Gwynn gold medal for exceptional achievement. For now, though, Finn needed to get home in time for Christmas. He caught the bus that afternoon, handed the baby over to his weeping mother, and slept fourteen hours a day in a state of convalescence like a soldier back from the trenches. His mother had already accepted the inevitable, particularly in light of the fact that Jack had fathered a girl. It was all Marianne's fault anyway, she said. The strap: an English Protestant with the morals of an alley cat, who had seduced Finn. Nothing could make Finn more sympathetic in the eyes of the parish, his mother added, than to take responsibility for a child abandoned by its mother.

He was seen as flawed, but noble. He knew that no such accommodations would have been made to a woman arriving home with a child. But, lonely and heartsick for Marianne, he took his comfort where he could.

Celia de Fréine

THE STORY OF ELIZABETH

'Skin an apple in one go, hang the peel above the door, and the first man in over the threshold is the man you'll marry.' So says Sister Mary Teresa of the Little Flower. And all of us in fifth class wait. To hear more customs, or pishogues as she calls them, from Kerry. The place she comes from. Kerry is where lots of mad things happen. It's where the people used to go around stabbing the cows of a Saturday night and draining the blood out of them. Not 'cos they were vampires but so as to pour it over their gruel for dinner the next day. 'Indeed, and the Kerry cows know Sunday,' is what Sister Mary Teresa says anytime she gets worked up.

She's worked up today. Halloween. Because she's spent too much time talking when she should be halfway through our history lesson. About the saints that are going to be murdered and have their monasteries plundered by the Vikings.

'Who came into your house when you threw the peel over the door, Sister?' Mary-Ellen yells from the back row.

''Twas a big old farmer.'

'Is that why you got married to Jesus?' Mary-Ellen shouts back.

'No, it is not. And before we start our lesson, have any of you girls got a proper question?'

Sister Mary Teresa says that every day. She's fed up with us asking about things that aren't important and has promised to give a special prize to the first girl who asks a proper question. None of us says anything.

'Very well,' Sister Mary Teresa says. 'Open your books at page forty-three.'

Mary-Ellen doesn't have a book. She doesn't have a schoolbag. Or the napkin we're supposed to have for wiping our hands after drinking our free milk and eating our free sandwiches, except on Wednesdays when we get a curranty bun. If truth be told, Mary-Ellen stole my napkin, in September, before we got Sister Mary Teresa for our teacher. And after I'd been asked over and over again why I had no napkin by the other nun, who wasn't as nice, I showed her where it was. Wrapped around Mary-Ellen's milk bottle. I knew it by the gold stripes on its border and the ivory sheen off its cloth. I wanted a white napkin. Or one that would turn white if Mammy washed it in Persil.

Mary-Ellen knows how to sing. Her favourite song is Panis Angelicus. That means bread of the angels. The nuns love listening to her belt it out in Latin. Mary-Ellen doesn't understand Latin, or Irish either, for that matter, but when Sister Mary Gabriel, the choir nun, heard her voice, she hammered the words into her. And Mary-Ellen learnt them off by heart.

I felt bad telling on her about the napkin. But it was my napkin that had been robbed. I didn't want to get whacked over the knuckles with a ruler. And I couldn't understand why someone who sings about angels could do something as mean as rob a napkin from someone who is almost as poor as she is.

Mary-Ellen lives in the soldiers' barracks up Biddy's Lane, past where we live in a flat. One of the aul ones in the flat upstairs said to me the other day, 'You couldn't be up to them children out of the barracks with their ginger hair. I'd steer clear of them if I was you.' But I like Mary-Ellen well enough. And her brother, Thomas, who's learning to be a plumber and her sister, Peggy, who works in the Swastika Laundry. Where they wash the sheets, except for the ones with flea shit on them.

I'm not allowed up the lane unless Mammy needs a pint of milk from Biddy's shop in a hurry. Like the day the milkman's horse dropped dead of a heart attack. That was when two boys chased after me on their go-kart and knocked me down and the bottle got smashed and all the milk flowed down the drain. Then Thomas came along and told the boys to lay off and bought me a new bottle off Biddy. Even though he didn't have an empty to give her. Me and Mary-Ellen had made up by then. I'd even bought her a gobstopper in Mr Wendy's.

Sometimes me and her go to the pictures in the Stella on Saturday. Mammy doesn't like me going 'cos she can't go herself. She has to stay home with my two brothers. Gregory who's going on for one and Dominick who's going on for two. But she lets me go when the film is about the Bible. Like last year when *Ben-Hur* was on and I told her the nun said we should go. Mammy had read about *Ben-Hur* in the paper.

'There's a fella from the North in that picture,' she said. 'Stephen Boyd. A Protestant. And the rest are Americans. Those stories are about the Jews. Are there no Jews left in Hollywood?' When I heard her say that, I was worried she wouldn't let me go, but in the end she gave me a shilling, ninepence to get in and thruppence to buy Honey-Bee sweets.

There was a new picture about the Bible in the Stella last week and I was let go to that as well. *The Story of Ruth.* Ruth's family are so poor her Daddy has to sell her to the Temple of Chemosh. Me and Mary-Ellen queued up early and got seats in the front row.

'How much did he get for her?' Mary-Ellen whispered.

'Six coins.'

'Are they one shillingses or two shillingses?'

'I can't see.'

We learnt a new word from the film: blemish. That's when a big bruise comes on your arm out of nowhere and you can't be sacrificed. Another girl has to take your place and she doesn't know the baldy fella in the purple dress is going to stab her through the heart with a dagger.

Me and Mary-Ellen walk home from school together but when we come to the bottom of our road I have to walk on ahead so Mammy doesn't see her. She doesn't approve of her anymore, not because she's out of the barracks but because she's two years older than me. I'm eleven and Mary-Ellen is thirteen. She started school late and was held back to do third class again. Last Monday Sister Mary Raphael said, 'That one is as thick as the wall.' That was the day all the girls except for Mary-Ellen had to be put out of the classroom and Sister Mary Teresa had to get a bucket and mop up a pool of watery blood under Mary-Ellen's desk that was like something you'd see on the floor of the pork butcher's. I had to go home on my own that day. When I asked Mary-Ellen which part of her was hurt she wouldn't tell me.

'Another year of this shite is all I have to put up with,' she says to me today. 'And then I'll be gone.'

'Gone where, Mary-Ellen?'

'To the Swastika Laundry, stupid. I'm gonna start the day I turn fourteen and if ever I pass you on the street I'll throw you a gobstopper 'cos my handbag is gonna be burstin' with them. And packets of fags. Have you ever smoked a fag?'

'No.'

'Come up Biddy's Lane tonight and I'll learn you how to smoke. There's gonna be fireworks. Thomas is gettin' a big box of them. Catherine wheels and rockets.'

Halloween is turning out to be great fun. I've learnt about apple peel and Kerry farmers and now I'm going to learn how to smoke. Mammy says it's important to listen to what people have to say 'cos, being from the North, she doesn't understand how things work in Dublin.

It's after half past six now and she's at the door talking to Mikey, the insurance man. He calls around every week to collect the money for our coffins for when we die 'cos if we didn't have insurance we'd be thrown into a pit with all the beggars. 'If that happened to me, I'd come back and haunt the graveyard man,' I said to Mammy last week. 'And frighten the shite out of him.'

'Don't let me hear words like from you that again, Veronica,' she said. 'It's that national school I blame. With its national brand. What kind of a country is this, anyway? At least they've stopped calling it the Free State. And well they might, what with the price of everything in it.'

'You're a scream, Mrs F.,' Mikey says, putting our money into his bag. 'From now on I'm going to call you The Lady of Shallot!'

Mammy likes talking to Mikey but he's taking so long she's afraid she'll miss *The Archers*. She had a bad cold last week and Mikey told her to boil a pot of onions and she'd be cured. They were special small onions called shallots. That's why he's calling her that. She boiled a big pot of them and there were so many I had to eat some as well even though I didn't have a cold. 'Just in case you get one,' Mammy said.

When Mikey's finished singing 'We'll gather lilacs in the spring again', Mammy goes down to the kitchen to get the book for Mikey to write our business in it. He leans over the wall, his bum in the air like a duck in the pond, and pinches a rose for his buttonhole off the bush that's rambling up from next door. While he's like that I make a run for it. Down the steps, along the path, out the gate and up the road as far as Biddy's Lane.

I've never been up Biddy's Lane after dark. And it really is dark in between the lamp posts. And smelly, like every cat in the city peed in it. It's spooky too. Like something out of one of Sister Mary Teresa's stories. I keep close to the wall so no one can see me and hope Mary-Ellen gets a move on. When I turn the corner I see the light from Biddy's shop. The houses in the barracks are lit up too. But there's no sign of fireworks and no one about, only Biddy, sitting behind her counter, staring out.

I'm sure she's just pretending to see out because when you're in a room that has the light on, looking out into the dark, you can see nothing. I know that from when Mammy tells me to keep an eye out for the rent man. After another few minutes there's still no sign of Mary-Ellen. I don't know whether or not to go back home. Mammy is sure to be mad at me and what's the point in being given out to when I've nothing to show for it? I decide to wait a little longer.

After a while I see Mary-Ellen sneaking out of a door at the far end of the barracks and coming up the lane towards me, carrying a shoebox in her arms. I shout, 'Mary-Ellen!'

She walks the other way, even though she must have heard me. I run after her. Just as she comes to the top of the lane, she turns.

'I can't do it,' she says.

'Do what, Mary-Ellen?'

A miaow comes out of the shoebox.

'What have you got in there? Kittens?'

'I can't do it.'

I look into the shoebox and there's a baby in it. Wrapped in newspaper. Small as the black doll, Bessie, I used to have, before Dominick broke her arms and legs off. The baby has streaks of blood on its chest and white stuff on its face like someone burst a giant bubble gum on its head.

'Where did you get it?'

'Swear you'll tell no one?'

'Cross my heart and hope to die.'

'It's me sister, Peggy's. She had it on the kitchen table. Me ma made her bite down on me da's belt so no one would hear her screamin' and yellin'.'

'Is your sister married?'

'Course not, stupid.'

'Why have you got the baby? Doesn't your sister want it?'

'Me Ma told me to get rid of it before anyone started askin' questions.'

'Get rid of it?'

'Stop askin' questions.'

The baby lets out a screech.

'We could bring it to the temple, Mary-Ellen. And sell it for six shillings.'

'What temple?'

'The one on Rathmines Road, before you come to the Stella.'

'That's not a temple. It's a bank. For rich people. We couldn't leave it there.'

Mary-Ellen starts to cry. A big snot comes out of her nose.

'I can't leave it here,' she says. 'A dog might get it.'

'We can't let a dog get it. Is it a boy or a girl?'

'A girl.'

'Tell you what, we can leave it at Biddy's.'

'Why?'

''Cos she has a telephone, stupid. And she can phone the guards. And they can come and get it. Her.'

'Biddy might see me,' Mary-Ellen says. 'She knows who I am. I'm always in there, gettin' fags for me da. Will you do it?'

'Do what? Leave the baby at Biddy's? No.'

'Why not, Veronica? What kind of a friend are you? You'll get no fags or gobstoppers off me when I start workin'.'

'I'll do it.'

'Do you want a fag now? I robbed one off me da.'

'No. How can I carry the baby and learn how to smoke at the same time?'

'I robbed it out of his jacket when he was in the back room, cursin' and swearin' and saying 'twas all Peggy's fault, the way she goes round with her arse burstin' out of her skirt.'

Mary-Ellen shoves the shoebox into my arms.

'What about the fireworks?'

'Thomas isn't back with them yet.'

'I'm gonna miss them.'

'Can't you come back later?'

'How? Biddy might recognise me.'

I walk back down the lane towards Biddy's. The baby is kicking her legs and turning her head from side to side. Her skin is pink and her hair is ginger like all of Mary-

Ellen's family. I sing her some of Mary-Ellen's hymn: 'O res mirabilis. Manducat Dominum. Pauper, servus et humilis.' She looks up at me and I bend over and kiss her on the forehead. When I get as far as the shop, I crawl under the window, reach up and turn the handle on the door and shove the shoebox in. Biddy screams: 'I'll have no squibs in my shop tonight.'

I run down the lane and, when I get to the end, turn and look back. There's no sign of Biddy. I bump into Mikey coming out of the house next door to ours.

'Where've you been?' he says. 'Your mother's worried sick. You're in for it now.'

He's right. When I get inside and tell Mammy I found a baby, she's very cross.

'Sweet Jesus the night! What did you do with it?'

'I shoved it in Biddy's door.'

'I hope no one saw you.'

'No one did, Mammy.

'Are you sure?'

'Yes.'

'What is it with you, Veronica? I can't let you out of my sight but you get into all kinds of bother. Last thing I want is to have the peelers knocking on our door.'

Mammy dries her hands on her apron and sits on the settee and asks me about the baby. I tell her about it, though I don't mention Mary-Ellen or her sister.

'It'll be on the news in the morning,' she says. 'I wonder what they'll call her?'

'What do you think they'll call her, Mammy?'

'Elizabeth, more than likely.'

'Why Elizabeth?

'Because they always pick the name of the saint whose feast day is on when they find a baby. And the next feast day of a woman saint is the fifth of November. Do you know how I know that?'

''Cos Elizabeth is your name, Mammy.'

'That's right. They'll probably baptise her straight away.'

'How'll they know she's a Catholic?'

'Everyone down here is a Catholic.'

'What will they do with her, Mammy?'

'Send her to the Home.'

'But she hasn't done anything wrong.'

'No, but somebody has.'

Mammy is so taken with the story she stops being cross. I pluck up the courage to ask her the question that's on the tip of my tongue.

'Mammy, do you know if there's a Temple of Chemosh in this country?'

'What kind of a place is that?'

'It's where you sell babies for six shillings.'

'Nobody sells babies. What kind of nonsense are they teaching you in that school?'

Before I can answer and tell her about the temple and how the girls in it get to wear lovely dresses and jewellery, she starts on one of her speeches: 'It's this country I blame. With its money that has harps and fishes on it. And that woman on the pound notes. I wouldn't mind but she's not even the queen of anything.' Mammy brushes her hair out of her eyes. 'Tell me this, did you learn any history today?'

'Yes, Mammy, we learnt about the Vikings.'

'What about the Fenians? Did you learn anything about the Fenians?'

'Not yet, Mammy.'

'Well, as soon as you do, I want to know all about them.'

'Why, Mammy?'

'Because when I was a wee girl like you, boys used to shout after me: 'Fenian, go home!'

'Why, Mammy?'

'I don't know. That's why I'm asking you. Will you ask the nun?'

'Yes, Mammy. Is there anything else you'd like to know?'

'That'll do for now. Off you go to bed and don't forget to say your prayers. The Temple of Chemosh, indeed!'

I kiss Gregory in his cradle made out of orange boxes and Dominick in the cot that used to be a clothes horse before he was born. And fold my gymslip over the bottom of my bed and climb in. I lie there, thinking about the baby who's going to be called Elizabeth and wondering why Mary-Ellen's sister had her on the kitchen table when she could have got the 15 bus to D'Olier Street and walked down O'Connell Street as far as the Rotunda Hospital. I keep repeating the word Mammy said to me over and over again: Fenians, Fenians, Fenians. And wonder about the special prize Sister Mary Teresa is bound to give me when I ask a proper question in class tomorrow.

Shauna Gilligan

The Window Overlooking the Chipper

The smell of disinfectant hung in the air of the long room, which was lit by a single strip of fluorescent light that ran from the door to the window, right where we needed it for our work. The rest of the room was bare, and I liked the way our voices echoed in the emptiness as we toiled through the evening and into the night, side by side at the large bay window overlooking the chipper, The Chick. When we leaned on the tips of our toes, we could just about see the glossy crown of a tree.

The baker rented the kitchen in the basement, the shopfront on the ground floor and this long room on the third floor. The landlord was good, he said, didn't overcharge on the rent but it was a pity the other floors weren't vacant. The first floor was living quarters and the second was split between a tanning salon and a solicitor's office. The queues out Declan Donuts during the day were not as big as those of The Chick at night, but fortunately the baker was still operating, unlike a lot of businesses around this area. He would have dearly loved to hire more people like us and produce more cakes, especially his famed carrot cake. He never used machines or took shortcuts in preparation. All the ingredients were prepared by hand: John checked that the raisins soaked in Hennessy were sufficiently plump and I grated the carrots. These were the two most important ingredients in baking, the baker said: moisture and the human touch.

John had once asked him about the name of the bakery, Declan Donuts, and he'd confessed he'd hoped that people would think it was like Dunkin' Donuts and rush inside. John had frowned and I was thinking, but you don't make donuts, and really, is Declan even your name? Maybe if the baker spent more time dropping batter into spitting oil instead of running up and down those stairs checking on us, he'd have a longer queue. But, of course, John didn't say anything, and I gave one of my vague smiles, as if I hadn't been listening, as if I didn't care.

Every Saturday the baker would roll the dice across the plastic table and whichever of us got the highest number wore the gloves. This evening I got a four and John got an eight.

'Sorry for your pretty hands,' the baker said reaching out as if to touch my hands but withdrawing before he did, like a turtle coming out for a peek.

'It's ok, the stains come out after a few days.'

The baker rubbed his hands together. 'Please try and get finished before three tonight. I've to have twenty-five carrot cakes ready by tomorrow.'

I caught his eye and a tremor crossed his face. He looked away and I turned my gaze to the carrots, at least six deep in the large crate.

'Yes, sir,' John said.

'On you go,' the baker said softly.

He nodded towards me before disappearing out the door.

John and I stood at the bay window, which was sealed shut. We listened to the silence the baker had left. Heat hung like a veil across the room. John ran his hand over his head that he'd shaved for a dare, then removed his army-green vest and apologised for doing so; I told him it was fine. I carefully rolled up the sleeves of my red silk kimono, worried momentarily that the baker might have tip-toed back up the stairs – he was always barefoot – and be on the other side of that door, listening to our idleness. I glanced out the window. The sky was still blue, the sun was still shining.

'See that blonde one in the queue?' John said, nodding towards the view of The Chick outside. 'Every time I look out the window, she's there.'

'She just queues to chat up the guy behind the counter. Can you see him without your glasses? The new one? He looks like Marlon Brando.'

John squinted into the distance. 'I can make out that he's got dark hair,' he said, 'lots of dark hair.'

'He's a fast worker. He goes through about two customers to the girl's one. Definitely on for employee of the month.'

Some nights The Chick was more entertaining than others.

'Ok, let's get going,' I said. 'Nothing much is happening there.'

John reached into a dirty navy satchel that looked like a schoolbag and pulled out two battered-looking red plastic cups. 'How about a drink? I should have done this before now but didn't want to scare you off.'

I took a cup from him. 'What are we drinking?'

'You'll see.' He reached into his bag again and produced a long thin bottle made of dark glass.

I leaned forward. 'That looks interesting.'

John eased the torn cork from the bottle. A clear, thick liquid slithered out, dropped into our grubby cups. I held the cup to my nose, sniffed it. There was no smell. He pulled out two curly straws from the bag.

'This way you'll be able to drink and work. And besides, it's just a pinch.' John indicated the dribble at the bottom of the cup. 'It's strong stuff.'

'The baker would be furious; you know it can't be a pinch if it's liquid.'

'Oh, shut up, Miss Carrot-Cake-of-the-Century.'

He play-punched me on the upper arm and I sucked through the yellow curly straw. My eyes smarted. What was this drink?

'Is this the stuff he uses for the raisins? The Hennessy?'

John gave me one of his sterner looks. 'Don't be stupid. I made it. I have a life outside of this room, you know.'

Over the course of the evening John removed his gloves again and again, pouring us larger and larger pinches of the clear liquid. I had the sensation of honey blooming in my mouth, hot and comforting. My voice no longer belonged to me and what came out of it was love. I wasn't even irritated by John constantly licking his lips and looking at me with that lopsided grin of his. The world was a beautiful place and the work I did was no more and no less significant than what Jesus did with water and wine.

My pile of grated carrots grew steadily.

'Want some water?'

John held out a glass – not plastic but real glass – but I shook my head. I'd have to go to the toilet to wash my hands, drink the water and then go back *again* to wash my hands. It was just too much trouble without a straw. I'd have liked if he'd held the glass to my lips but I felt if I were to ask him to do that, he would take it as a sign that I wanted to be intimate with him. That was not the case. I was taken, you could say. At a push, I could happily lie with the Marlon Brando lookalike from The Chick, maybe, or perhaps Matt Damon, who was once rumoured to be living nearby, but not the man feeding me potentially lethal alcohol.

Besides, I thought John looked better with his glasses and he hardly wore them anymore. The baker had discovered a trick. Knowing when a raisin is plumped enough is by touch, so John's work was far more accurate when he went by feel rather than by sight. Over the last year John had worked for the baker, the best results were gained on the evenings when he did not wear his glasses. I continued grating, my hands stained with carotene. I turned my head from side to side, stretching out my neck, damp in the heat. I sucked the last of the liquid from the red plastic cup. I listened to John gulp down the water. He was lucky to have those sheer blue gloves and now he wouldn't have a hangover later.

I examined my pile of grated carrots. It was huge. But I'd hardly made a dent in the wooden crate filled with carrots. I glanced at John's work. One metal bowl was nearly full – these were the correctly plumped raisins and the other, smaller one, had just a handful of raisins that needed more soaking. I couldn't see inside the pot that sat on the floor beside him, but he dipped his ladle in and brought out the gleaming fruit so frequently I guessed he'd be done before me.

'What about that couple?' I said, nodding at two men who had reached the top of the queue in The Chick. 'Do you think they're happy?'

John squinted into the distance again. 'I guess so ...' He cleared his throat. 'Why,' he asked, 'why won't any of them look up to the window and see us? Notice that we're here?'

'They're busy. But just because they're holding hands it doesn't mean they're happy. I've had lots of boyfriends who insisted on holding my hand too tightly and it was, if I'm honest, what brought the relationships to a sorry end.'

I blinked and a tear rolled out of the side of my eye.

'Are you crying?'

'No.'

A rush of warmth spread through my entire body. My hands worked faster with the large carrot, transforming it into moist flecks of tastiness. I emptied the contents of the baby blue container into the large metal bowl. I reached down and picked up another carrot and began again.

'You are. You're crying.' John laughed. 'You're in love!'

I grated the carrot back and forth back and forth. Something was bubbling in my throat. Again, I emptied the contents of the baby blue container into the large square metal bowl, reached down and picked up another carrot. I grated back and forth, back and forth. I felt metal against my knuckles, heard the scrape, scrape, scrape, felt the pain.

John put a sheer-blue-gloved hand on my arm. 'Stop.'

I stopped grating, willing my shaking hands to be still.

'Look at them, look at those men.' John nodded at the window.

I looked out and the men were no longer holding hands. They were embracing and kissing. Brown bags fat with food dangled from their clutches.

'I thought you couldn't see properly without your glasses.'

John sighed. 'I can make out shapes and what they're doing, it's only the detail that I miss.'

I sniffed. I was in love, that much was true. But I was also not in love.

'Allow me?'

John had taken off his gloves and was standing with a tissue in his hands. I looked down into the bowl of shining carrot flecks. I turned my face towards him. He wiped slowly, and so very gently that I began to cry again.

'It's ok,' he said, still wiping. 'It's ok, it's what you're made of.'

I quietened down, listened to John's humming as he cleaned.

'There.' He stood back and admired his work. 'You look as pretty as the day before you worked here.' He threw the mascara smudged tissue in the bin, slipped his hands back inside the gloves. 'Come on, let's get finished. See? The queue is nearly gone.'

He was right. The queue at The Chick had dwindled to seven people; it must be after one in the morning. A wave of tiredness came over me. I reached back into the crate for the last carrot. My fingers roamed blindly and when I felt a spider crawling on me, I didn't scream – what was the point, really – instead I gently shook it off. Company was always welcome. Tenderness always needed. I pulled out the last carrot. The last one is always the slowest, like the body knows that the trial has come to an end and resigns.

I thought about what John had said, that I was as pretty as the day before I worked here. How long had I been working here? Six, nine, ten months? I smiled sadly, recalling a time when all my days were filled with idleness. I remembered the evening I queued at The Chick for fish and chips simply because there was nothing decent on television. I'd looked up at this building on the other side of the street. It was in complete darkness except for the red and yellow neon light above the wooden door spelling out the name Declan Donuts. A few stories up, framed by the bright light behind him, a man stood at a window, gazing down at me with a most beautiful smile. I waved up at him and his smile grew, and his eyes opened fully. He looked majestic. But I had reached the top of the queue and turned to place my order, and when I looked back up at the window, the man was gone.

I took my chips and my fish, and I walked across the street and stood beneath the neon sign eating, wondering who Declan was and what his donuts were like. I felt a tap on my shoulder. It was the man who had smiled at me from the window. I stared at him. He wore black dungarees and a cotton scarf which covered his head and was tied back at the nape of his neck, giving him an air of strangeness. I wondered at his bare feet but said nothing.

'You're not looking for a job, are you?'

I *was* looking for a job. I was, if I could admit it, looking for everything. How could he have known? I nodded, and followed him up flights of stairs that curled beautifully below inviting ceilings, leading us higher and higher. He brought me into a room where another man sat plucking something from one bowl and placing it into another.

'You'll work with John here,' he said, 'and start tomorrow, Saturday.'

John squinted at us through thick black-framed glasses and smiled, and I returned his smile. Then he bent his head low in concentration. I stared at the window, saw how the light was bright and inviting.

'I've been grating alongside John but the whole process is slowing me down. I need someone' – he stared at my hands – 'with a lighter touch than I. Someone with warmth. Like you.'

Then he indicated for me to follow him and we went down all those stairs, further now, into the back of the building, into the basement kitchen. He pointed to a large bin in the corner into which I stuffed the brown paper bag with leftover chips and the remains of the fish. He nodded towards the sink and I washed my hands. I took the blue paper towel he held out for me and dried them. He walked over to the industrial fridge and opened it, taking out a tray filled with tiny squares of cake.

When he placed into my mouth the most exquisite carrot cake I had ever tasted, I knew.

'Yes?' He nodded eagerly at me. 'You come tomorrow?'

'Yes.' I nodded. 'Oh! This cake is just so ...'

He held out his hands and I placed mine onto his. He bowed and said in a soft voice, 'The cake is everything.'

He closed his fingers, one by one over my hands, and squeezed. I wanted to speak, but my mind was filled with something trying to untangle itself. He leaned in towards me, took my long hair from my shoulders and gently placed it down my back. My heart seemed to leap.

He whispered in my ear. 'Shhh, my pretty one, calm.'

He led me back outside, onto the street, still holding one hand. He swung me around, as if we were going to dance. I found myself reaching up and running my fingers over the lids of his beautiful dark eyes, searching. It was like I had come home, I remember that feeling, as if I had returned after a long journey.

Now that we'd finished our work, John and I stood side by side looking out the window, waiting for the baker to return. In silence we leaned forward, anchoring ourselves against the table, and looked onto the crown of the tree, bushy and green. Then we stood back on the flats of our feet and watched the bleary-eyed owners of The Chick pull down the shutters and click the padlock into place. A streetlight flickered in the darkness.

Antonia Hart

SOLE TRADER

For the better part of five years, I researched and wrote about Irish women in business in the nineteenth century. I was doing a PhD in history and tumbled overboard, gladly, as you must. Usually, when I told people what I was doing, they asked who I had found, or held my forearm while they filled me in on a woman from their own family who had run the dairy, or the hotel, or been the one to keep the farm solvent after a husband, brother, or father had died, gone to America, or taken to the bed. There was a lot of it about, which was more or less the conclusion of my PhD.

I loved hearing these stories, and the fact that they were told, but it wasn't until after I had submitted that I gave any thought to my own family history. The story is ordinary, as they all are. Christina Brennan and Patrick Hart married each other on an August Sunday in 1875 in the cool dark of St Mary's Pro-Cathedral in Marlborough Street, on the north side of Dublin city. Christina came to the church from home, across the broad thoroughfare of Sackville Street, usually a hectic shopping street, quiet on the weekly day of rest. Home, on the far side of Sackville Street, in the heart of Dublin's markets district, was, for Christina, Moore Street Market: a tiny, granite-flagged street of a dozen shops, accessed through a redbrick arch between two buildings on Moore Street. Patrick lived in Riddall's Row, around the corner. Their families followed two of the traditional trades of the markets: the Brennans were fishmongers, and the Harts were butchers. Generation after generation of both families had followed the family trades, repeatedly moving premises but always staying hard by home, an area delineated by Great Britain Street (now Parnell Street) to the north and Henry Street to the south. Unsurprisingly, the market people formed a community in which families were intertwined by marriage, by shared living spaces, and by helping one another at work, and with each other's children.

Christina and Patrick were typical, both in choosing a match from among the people they had known all their lives and in marrying at the Pro-Cathedral. St Mary's, known in its early days as 'the chapel' and later as 'the Pro', was a city landmark, featured on picture postcards of the capital, and the location for all kinds of national celebrations, commemorations, and state funerals. Despite its grandeur, there was nothing aspirational in a couple from the markets choosing it for their wedding. It was also the parish church of the market traders. There, all the neighbours, friends, and family members who surrounded Christina and Patrick attended weekly Mass, observed holy days of obligation, made their First Communions and Confirmations, lit candles for the souls of the faithful departed, prayed for causes close to their hearts, married, baptised their babies and buried their dead. The patterns of family and community were clear, and for the young couple, home, work, love, worship, and marriage all followed paths traced by their parents and grandparents.

As newlyweds, Christina and Patrick lived in Great Britain Street, and Patrick continued his work as a butcher. They moved house three or four times within a few years, mostly up and down the same street, never straying further than two minutes' walk from home, and ending up in the tightly-wedged familiarity of 13 Moore Street Market. Less than a year after their August wedding, Christina, now twenty-three, gave birth to a son, named, as were both her husband and her father, Patrick. In March 1878, a sister followed: Julia Mary. But in October 1879 Christina received a message that her husband had had an accident: he had fallen 'off a car' and been taken to the Richmond Hospital, where he had died from injuries to his head. Christina had probably already suspected, by the time she got this terrible news, that she was pregnant again. She gathered her two toddlers and possessions to move them next door to number 12, another small house, with three rooms and one window at the front. Navigating these dimensions was second nature to Christina, and she squeezed everyone in.

Moore Street Market meant a crowded living space, but also the convenience of family help. Christina's father, Patrick Brennan, was at the top of the street at number 3, and her sister-in-law Mary Hart was an opposite neighbour. It was Mary who ran across the street and upstairs to lend a hand when Christina went into labour on 5 March 1880. She was there when Edward was born later that day. Christina would have been still uncomfortable from the birth, still bleeding and swollen, when, three weeks after Edward was born, Julia, just turned two, showed signs of sickness: the dreaded rough rash, sore throat, and high temperature that turned out to be contagious scarlatina, scarlet fever. Julia declined rapidly. Mary was on hand again, to help out with nursing, but within seven days Julia was dead.

In the space of six months, Christina's life changed completely. She lost her husband, her home and her daughter, and had to decide how to provide for herself and her two small sons, one still a suckling newborn. Unexpected widowhood, and death resulting from childhood illness were of course much more common in the nineteenth century than they are now, but that kind of loss lands with a force that is not determined by how many other people have felt something similar. What were her feelings? They are unrecorded. Brought low by grief, maybe ill with it, while also consumed with fear for her surviving children, and in a state of constant anxiety about money and the future? Whatever feelings crawled or swept through her, she took action, and did so in her own and her sons' best interest. Any child of the markets grew up familiar with a parent's trade, and for Christina, fishmongering was what she had witnessed and helped out with all her life. Now she set herself up as a fishmonger and brought her boys up in Moore Street Market, in the pattern of her own youth.

From then on, Christina worked as a fishmonger and lived in the same street as her father, eventually moving into his house with her two boys. But she did not surround the boys solely with Brennan fishmongers. There were Hart family members all around them, in Riddall's Row, Coles Lane, Norfolk Market and of course Moore Street Market itself, where Mary and another Edward were. The Harts were usually butchers, and, confusingly, were usually called Patrick, Edward, or Joseph, Julia or Mary, so as they grew up, Christina's sons heard their own names, their sister's and their father's echoing around the lanes. Proximity to their father's family also meant proximity to the other family trade. By the time Christina was forty-five, and Patrick and Edward were in their early twenties, they were both working as butchers. Christina, supported by her own family and her in-laws, had helped them to navigate their way to adulthood, and to learn a trade that could and did yield an excellent living. The money they made later, still as relatively young men, enabled both brothers to move out of the congested markets area of their childhood and bring up their own families surrounded by the space and sea air, generous gardens, and substantial houses of the Howth Road. They continued the rather suffocating family tradition of living on top of each other, buying houses not half a mile apart. Their businesses were even closer. Patrick opened his own shop in Moore Street, and Edward his in Great Britain Street. Christina watched as her grandchildren grew up in comfort, and her sons developed lives which looked more middle-class than her own. They no longer lived over the shop, but out of the city. They sent their children to smart schools. They ordered bespoke clothes, employed help in the house and gardeners to keep the view pleasant. But none of that was for Christina. She stayed in the same square half-mile of the city centre every one of her eighty-seven years and died there in 1932, in a room above Patrick's Moore Street shop.

Christina Hart was my great-grandmother, her youngest child Edward, my grandfather. My father grew up in the bay-windowed house on the Howth Road which was Edward's retreat from the city centre. What intrigues me most about Christina's life is the idea of her, still in her twenties, facing into widowhood and single motherhood, evaluating her skills and resources and wondering how to convert them into a means of footing the family bills until her boys could earn their own livings. Setting up as a sole trader or in business was something many thousands of women did, and in this, as in so many respects, Christina's story was a common one. Unless you came from a family well enough off to support you as an adult, or you married someone who made enough money to keep both of you, you had to earn your living, and often this meant supporting a child or an infirm parent as well. While nineteenth-century Irish society was not exactly set up to favour women's enterprise, if you had pressing financial issues then you couldn't necessarily stop to consider whether or not it was considered respectable for you to turn your front room into a shop, or to open your house to boarders. You were one of the lucky ones if you had a front room to convert, a house to use.

Christina was lucky, too, in that she had an accessible trade. Her success was modest by some metrics. She didn't rise to the top of the fish business and produce, from nothing but her own abilities and pair of chapped and reddened hands, a life of comfort for her family, and leave the smelly market lanes behind. She could have chosen to, later, but that was not what she wanted. Although it had familiarity to recommend it, the three-roomed house in Moore Street Market sounds like a cramped wreck of a place, in a dilapidated, overcrowded and unsanitary street. But feeding, clothing and housing your family, and bringing up two healthy children to a trade by which they could support themselves, was an achievement. By that measure, Christina was successful. As a self-employed person, a sole trader, you backed yourself. You touted for business, you provided the goods or services, you managed money in and out, you made nothing when you couldn't work because a child was sick or a migraine meant you could hardly turn your head on the pillow. Setting yourself up, from a most modest base, in a society designed to prefer men, was a challenge, but Christina wasn't anywhere near the only woman in Ireland to meet it. She wasn't even the only woman in Moore Street Market to meet it.

A snapshot of Moore Street Market after the century turned, on census night, 1901, shows the working lives of Christina's neighbours. The street, so small and insignificant, despite its endless commercial churn, that it was not even listed in Thom's Directory, was almost deserted. By then it held fifteen buildings, each with a shopfront, and only five, including Christina's, were inhabited. Ten vacant buildings in any street will lend a depressing air. When ten equates to two-thirds of a commercial street, it's a definite dampener. But Christina's neighbours couldn't afford to spend time moping about the atmosphere. Immediately next door, in a house later occupied by Christina's brother-in-law Edward Hart and his family, was Patrick Gannon. Gannon was a baker, and his wife, Margaret, was a shopkeeper. On the other side, in number 4, widow Honor Cullen was a clothier, another traditional trade of Moore Street Market. Her adult children lived with her, as Christina's did. In number 5, Thomas Meehan was a coal labourer, sixty-eight years old and surely hoping some kind of retirement was in sight. The last occupied house, number 6, was home to Mary Doyle, also a widow, aged forty. Mary Doyle appears in the census as the rare feminine 'butcheress', and her uncle, living with her, appears as a butcher's assistant, suggesting that the balance of power in the Doyle house was tilted in Mary's favour. Each of these women, Margaret Gannon, Christina Hart, Honor Cullen and Mary Doyle, had a trade that enabled her to work for herself, whatever working for herself might look like. She might have set up a small business, in a built shop with an employee, she might have run an outdoor stall single-handedly, or she might have walked the streets with a basket of wares, calling as she went.

In Christina's daily life, she saw women working for themselves, doing business in the local economy and employing others. In the market streets, the traders lived and worked on top of one another, selling second-hand clothes, shoes, and furniture, as well as fresh fruit and vegetables. The butchers who later proliferated in Moore Street were now concentrated in Riddall's Row, where their presence meant a constant throughput of live animals into the many slaughterhouses of the back lanes, intensifying the smell, the refuse, and the noise. The piled-up stalls and shops of the markets, the lime-splashed yards, the heaps of rubbish, were only minutes from the premium shops and luxury hotels of Sackville Street, still then the capital's finest thoroughfare. Not unusually for a capital city, privilege and precarity lived cheek by jowl. In Sackville Street and its environs, just as in Moore Street Market, women earned their own livings and ran their own businesses. From Christina's house in Moore Street Market to Nelson's Pillar was, if you were dawdling, a three-minute walk. The tram terminus was at the Pillar, where people from outlying suburbs like Kingstown, Rathmines and Howth alighted and hived off, ready to do business of one kind or another in the city centre. They hurried to offices and shops, to work or to carry out errands, to meet a friend or lover for lunch or tea, attend a political meeting, pawn a ring. A fifteen-minute stroll took Christina from the Pillar down Sackville Street, left at Eden Quay, where, if you hadn't already picked it up, the smell of the river hit you, left again up Marlborough Street, past the Pro-Cathedral, and back along North Earl Street towards the Pillar again. Women's businesses were visible all the way along, and perhaps looked more like businesses here than they did in the half-abandoned clutter of Moore Street Market.

Christina's disposable income is likely to have been minimal and occasional, but whatever she had she could have spent in all kinds of businesses run by women. Walking the loop from Nelson's Pillar to river to Pillar again in 1894, she would have passed a woman's business on average every thirty seconds. She could have ordered a dress; bought the new longline corset; gone to a different establishment for breakfast, lunch, tea, and dinner; bought something to relieve a headache, along with soap, toilet water, and a hot water bottle; booked a room for the night; bought wine, whiskey, cigarettes, and a newspaper; filled her shopping basket with provisions and chosen a bag of sweets. When she couldn't stretch from one end of the week to the next, she could have borrowed from a pawnbroker: from Margaret Lowry in Marlborough Street or any of the women brokers in Summerhill, Gardiner Street and North King Street. She could have transacted with any of these women and been home in ten minutes. It doesn't mean it was easy to be a woman running your own show, but it does mean it was common. All around Christina, women offered the ordinary necessities of family life: food, fuel, clothes, medicine, furniture, boots, credit. Maybe she didn't give them a second thought, as she cut and cleaned her fish, slapped it into appealing displays, priced and wrapped it. She did know they were there, though. They were her neighbours, members of her family and her husband's, friends, people she saw at Mass. They were in and of Christina's world and they, and similar women outside and beyond it, are the answer to the question 'Who have you found?'

Phyl Herbert

THE PRICE OF SILENCE (*extract*)

'Shall I Be Mother?'
It was like preparing for a first date.
It was like being born again.
It was like getting a second chance.

It is Saturday, the second day of October, 1993. The time is 2.30 p.m. The place, the Davenport Hotel, Dublin.

What do I say to her when we meet? Do I hug her? No, that would be too invasive altogether. This girl doesn't know me and I don't know her. The fact that I happened to know her intimately for six weeks – the first six weeks of her twenty-six years – doesn't give me permission to assume any degree of familiarity. I will hand over the first moments to her.

What will I wear? I allow myself to think a lot about what I might wear for this first meeting. I desperately want to appear in the best light possible. A well-fitted pale-blue trouser suit and a white blouse – all bought for the occasion – would look suitably understated. Black ankle boots rimmed with a red trim would soften the business-like image.

James, our social worker, had told me that the correct term now is 'birth mother'. At first I was uncomfortable with it, but now I understand the usage better. After all, I had only known Elizabeth for those precious few weeks. My part in her life had been to give birth to her, to bring her into a safe environment. Then to set her off on the river of life.

I set off to meet my daughter.

How will she view what I had done to her? A thousand questions are bubbling up inside me now, demanding answers. What sort of life did she live? What were her parents like? Did she have good friends, and was she in a relationship? I know, ultimately, that I will have to silence my curiosity for the moment, just allow Elizabeth to share whatever comes naturally to her.

It is a sunny day as I walk through the door, my first time ever to visit this new Dublin hotel. Immediately, I regret not having paid a visit earlier to familiarise myself with the layout. The marble floor at the reception area shimmers like water at low tide, and the sound of my new boots on this hard surface sends a shock wave through my body. The next few steps feel like wading through an incoming tidal current. For a moment I think I have lost my footing.

And then I see her. She is sitting with James. I had completely forgotten him – how did I do that? He is here for the initial introductions. He is sitting with his back to me, facing Elizabeth, who is now looking at me with a fixed gaze that says, *Who is this woman coming towards me?*

James stands up and steps backwards, allowing me to come nearer. It is like walking into a magnetic field, an invisible ley line marking the place between us. The words exchanged in those first few seconds don't register at all.

Words don't seem to matter, because for now we are both in a place beyond mere language. We are looking at each other now for the first time in twenty-six years. James glances from me to Elizabeth. Then, after a quick greeting ceremony, he leaves us.

'How are you?' are the first words I hear.

Elizabeth looks at me carefully, taking in the features of my face. A slow smile spreads across her beautiful mouth, lighting up those clear blue eyes.

'I'll order. Tea or coffee?'

My stomach is churning. 'Tea, please.'

The waitress brings the tea and sets the tray down in front of us. A ray of sunshine beams over the auburn head of the young woman opposite me. I study her slender hands as she pours the tea and the elegant way she lifts her cup. I need to say something but I feel tongue-tied. Every word that rises up in my throat I push down again. I take a deep calming breath.

'So, when did you arrive in Dublin?'

She takes a sip of tea.

'Yesterday. My brother and his family live near you, actually.'

Suddenly, the noise of massed male voices around us swamp our words. A group of people have gathered to watch an international rugby match.

'Let's go somewhere else,' Elizabeth says.

We step outside into the fresh air and laugh together. The ice is well and truly broken. She looks across at me. 'I wanted to contact you earlier, to say we could meet somewhere else, before James arrived. Maybe in the Mont Clare Hotel across the road. Then I realised I didn't have your number.'

We walk slowly towards Nassau Street. I notice we are the same height, shoulder to shoulder.

'Let's go somewhere quiet,' she says. 'You know Dublin better than me.'

She places her hand on my shoulder and I feel another surge of affection towards her. It is like the roles are reversed. I am being looked after, not by a daughter, but someone very close, almost like a sister.

'The Westbury,' I reply. 'It's always quiet there.'

We find a corner, over by a window, with plush green armchairs. We sit side by side, a low table in front of us, looking out onto a side street. This time I order, and ask Elizabeth if she'd like something to eat. But we are both too preoccupied to really think of our appetites.

'Tell me about yourself.'

Elizabeth laughs. 'I've told you most of the main details in that long letter James asked both of us to write. The only thing that has changed is that I've finished with my boyfriend. And I've at last met you.'

She reaches towards me and holds my hand. She holds it for what seems like a long time.

I open my handbag and reach into it. 'I have something here for you.' I pass her the box. It is a door knocker in the shape of a Claddagh ring, one heart held by two hands. 'Just in case you don't want to meet me again.'

She looks at me as if I've said something shocking. 'We've only just met and you're thinking of *abandoning me again?*'

'I didn't mean it that way, Elizabeth, the door knocker means you can call on me anytime. I will always be there for you.' I trail off into a stream of babbling words, thinking how silly my present and how foolish my words. A pang of guilt at my artless ramblings renders me tongue-tied. I wasn't there for her for the past twenty-six years and she is here now for me. She is the brave soul, the one showing maternal compassion.

When Elizabeth breaks into a big smile, I know all is not lost. That deep chasm may still be there but now the air between us is humming with possibilities.

'It's beautiful! Of course I'll want to see you again.'

The waitress brings our tea and again Elizabeth takes control.

'I won't say shall I *be mother.*' Her eyes light up again. They are a very definite shade of blue and I think of the mysteries of genetics, because both Brian and myself have hazel eyes.

'Isn't it a coincidence that we are both teachers?' She tells me about her university job where she lectures in the women's studies department.

'I will be in Dublin again soon, Phyl. Can we meet then?'

This is not the end, I tell myself. It is only the beginning of the beginning. I listen carefully to the gentle ebb and flow of her voice as she tells me about her brother's children, her only niece and nephew. I think of my numerous nieces and nephews and wonder if she'll ever meet them. Her voice is nothing like mine or Brian's. A few months later, when I meet her parents, I discover that she speaks exactly like her mother.

Two weeks later we meet again, this time in the Gresham Hotel. Elizabeth has spent the day at a women's studies conference in UCD. She is elated at meeting so many academics and listening to so many papers from so many Irish and UK universities. We find a quiet corner in the lounge and order our drinks.

'So good to see you.' She reaches out, takes my hand and holds it tightly. 'I've been thinking about you so much.'

The drinks arrive – two glasses of Heineken. We clink our glasses. Now I notice that when she smiles, the contours of her face dimple in exactly the same way as

Brian's. I am besotted with this beautiful, intelligent girl sitting beside me.

'It's like I've found that piece of the puzzle I'd lost. And now here you are!' Elizabeth beams at me.

'I can say the very same thing,' I reply. Her openness delights me, and the sound of her voice enchants me. I'm hypnotised by her very presence. 'How was your conference, Elizabeth?'

'Superb. It's fascinating to hear of other people's research studies.'

I am curious to know what her area of research is and I ask her.

'Nature and nurture. I have many friends who are like me. When I started school, two of my best friends were adopted and I thought then that everybody was.'

We are on our third glass of Heineken when she puts down her glass and, in a serious voice says, 'Phyl, you were robbed.'

I am puzzled. I don't know how to respond. What is her line of thinking? The sudden switching of tracks confuses me. I look at her and I see that her entire face has changed and I can almost see the little baby that I knew in St Patrick's Mother and Baby Home.

'Why didn't you keep me?'

This is a huge question. I should have prepared a proper answer but I am guilty of presuming that she would have known all the answers. That she understood that for me to have kept and reared her then would have brought shame on my family. It would have made both of us outcasts in society, as society existed then. I want to say that it is something I will explain at a later stage. That I know it isn't a trick question and that she needs a serious answer. She has already told me that during her university studies she wrote essays on the subject of why young girls handed up their children for adoption. She quotes some of those facts now. In 1967, the year of her birth, 97 per cent of babies born to unmarried women in Ireland were given up for adoption. She is included in this stark statistic. What she is really asking me, of course, is not why I had abandoned her, as a general sociological sort of question, but how I, personally, could have done such a thing. No, this isn't an academic question at all. This is a question from a real person – my own daughter.

I think carefully before speaking. A few misspoken words could do a lot of damage now.

'It was only weeks after I left St Patrick's that the reality of what I had done came crashing down on me.' I pause a moment to let that sink in. 'I rang up the convent and asked for my baby. I told them I wanted you back. The nun on the phone let me ramble on a bit. Then she said, calmly and clearly, that if I didn't stop whingeing she would leave you on my mother's doorstep the following morning.'

'I understand, I do. I really do.' Elizabeth says, but somehow I feel, deep down, that she doesn't really. That the words don't connect with her. Don't convince her.

A distance has clearly been created between us now, after my feeble, fumbled explanation. Still, I feel I owe her a further explanation. At a later stage I will try to tell her the truth: that there would have been no room for her in my family home. Not only because it was an overcrowded house, but because she would have been exposed as she grew up to a hostile and toxic world. Nor do I tell her that I gazed into the face of every little girl I saw for years after parting with her to see if I could find some resemblance to her. That I was like a detective looking for clues in every family setting that was new to me.

In silence, we take a taxi together outside the hotel. Elizabeth is staying with her brother, who lives not too far from my own rented accommodation. She tells me later that when she was getting out of the taxi, the driver asked her if she and her girlfriend had a good night on the town. She replied that this was no girlfriend but her own mother. The man, too, fell silent.

The next time I hear from Elizabeth she asks me if I'd like to meet her mother. The request throws me into a state of panic. I am not ready to meet her mother. Not yet, anyway. Why is Elizabeth rushing things? Her words – 'You were robbed' – are still haunting me.

Patricia Hickey

STRAW

She sits at the table beneath the tree gazing upwards, her eyes pale beneath the livid sky. Seashells are suspended on strings from the branches, their fading colours catching the light, the clacking sounds as they collide like agitated birds. More shells lie on the table in front of her, awaiting the slop and splash of her paints.

'Shall I thread them for you?'

Bernie withdraws her gaze from the tree and turns as her companion speaks.

'No thanks, Moira, I prefer to paint them and let them dry first. Oh, look, some of them have no holes. How will I thread them?'

Moira pauses at the petulant note in her friend's voice. She looks at the shells, like miniature sun hats, some with holes at the peak. She had called them Chinese hats as a child, believing that diminutive people lurked in the sandhills along the beach, waiting for her departure before donning the tiny hats once she was out of sight. Bernie reaches for the paint and a red oval oozes onto a saucer. Her head is bent low, uncomfortably so, Moira thinks, pondering if this too is part of her friend's dementia.

'I would like a Quab, please.'

'A what? A Quab, did you say? What in heaven's name is that?'

Bernie remains silent, sitting back into her wicker chair, and Moira thinks that her straw hat looks a bit wicker too. Straw lady, she thinks; her friend is slowly turning into straw. Perhaps she means Cob, mud and straw mixed together in earlier times to make houses.

'Do you mean Cob? Are you planning on building something?'

She hears her over-reaching attempt to make sense of the nonsense. She knows that Bernie will spot it.

'Why would I want to use anything as messy as mud? We are about to eat, you know. I mean a Quab. You will want one too, when I explain.'

'First of all you need a teapot, filled to the brim with freshly made tea. On top of the pot you place a saucer, then a teacup, then another saucer and on top of that a coffee cup filled with coffee, on top of which is placed a plate of sandwiches, then a plate of cakes.'

Bernie commences to create an imaginary tower that she weaves in the air with her hands, an arrangement that Moira realises is a literal high tea. She watches as her hands, stick-like, sinewy and pale, insert her creation into the space between them. She does not mention that the sandwiches will get squashed, nor that the arrangement does not work at the top of the tower. She notes the inclusion of coffee. Moira dislikes tea.

'And that,' says Bernie, leaning back in her chair, 'is a Quab.'

Moira checks the word later and discovers that it is a middle-English word for a bog. Bernie never studied languages in college; her thing was archaeology, but still ... It all smacks of a performance for Moira. She recalls their days dabbling in amateur dramatics and Bernie's interpretation of *A Doll's House*, which must have sent Ibsen spinning in his grave. She had always been something of a failed Thespian in her youth, delivering the defining statement on any given situation. They had visited the Céide Fields once, when she was still an archaeology student. She had talked at length in the coach that took them to the site, about the buried field system that lay beneath a covering of blanket bog. She sprinkled the account with technical terms, about probing with long metal rods to locate the concealed field walls, about pollen analysis and coaxial field layout. Bernie's persona expanded before her eyes as she entered into this imagined space, so that it became a subterranean Hy-Brasil for the listeners as she spoke. She claimed this space alongside the prehistoric inhabitants, dividing up their land into neat shapes; but there was no mention then of Cobs, or even of a Quab. They were bitten all over by midges as they clamoured across the site and tried to imagine what lay buried beneath their feet.

Moira turns her head slightly to check on Bernie. Her companion sits quietly, smiling up into the tree. They decide to have tea and scones and move indoors to the kitchen, the fantastical Quab forgotten. Bernie's English schooling causes her to use the clipped *o* in scone, so that Moira hears 's'gone' and averts her gaze as her friend overstuffs her mouth with the crumbly dough.

They used to argue in their youth, in what Moira believes now was another life, one that, even then, was not truly their own. Debates, their arguments might be called, more accurately, but they got pretty heated at times. And now, when she thinks about them again, she wonders how much of her real self was in them. She tries to recall the themes: something to do with women's rights, no doubt, as everything was then. What she recalls is the exhaustion from all the consciousness-raising, as they shed the expectations of others for their exfoliated and depilated bodies. And all the while the men went about their own self-discovery, banging on drums for hours in the woods – or so they would have them believe – as they tried to make contact with their inner maleness. Well, that was always good for a laugh! But she had wondered at the time about their relentless exclusion of the men, recalling Bernie's scoffing dismissal of her reservations. That sneering putdown was a habit that had always irritated her, a habit that her friend had retained over the years. She realises with a shock that Bernie no longer scoffs.

She decides that they were arguments for the sake of it, as they went about the task of inventing themselves. But of course she could not see that then. She was too busy trying to figure out who or what she was as she inched forward, argument by argument, with her life.

She detects a movement beyond the window. Bernie's husband is engaged in some invented garden chore. He keeps out of contact with them these days as they all go about their conjured activities. Moira thinks that he is avoiding his wife's decline. He bends low and firms some newly planted saplings into the soil with his boot. His wife likes trees. She finds it strange that Bernie found a man that she wanted to take into her self-contained world. And somehow that was how it had continued for them, separate, yet together. Moira had long ago abandoned the attempt to understand their relationship, but she remained grateful that Bernie had left some space for her. She watches as he stands back and studies the saplings, his eyes focused on the topmost branches. He remains there for some time, motionless.

Right now she has set up yet another arrangement on a table – she can hardly call it a still life, for it is really a scattering of random objects. It is vivid with colour, for Bernie likes colour. The plants and plates and bowls that litter the space are interspersed with shells, for her friend must have shells. Moira has added some large cowries, on loan from her own collection. These curling shapes had decorated her bathroom, implying an interesting life in the South Seas but which she thinks hint at unsavoury links with pirates. She hopes her friend will attempt to paint some of the objects. A sheet of paper and an array of paints, jars and brushes are spread in front of her, but Bernie is looking beyond the table towards a birdfeeder stuck onto the window. A large magpie straddles the feeder, glaring into the room

'Water, I forgot water.' Moira takes one of the jars and moves towards the kitchen.

The two friends had inched forward with their lives throughout their youth, as if trying them on for size. They danced at discos in local rugby clubs, posing against damp walls, feigning indifference to the teenage boys with exaggerated quiffs and sweaty hands, as they walked along in front of them in an endless inspection. They ventured into side street cafés with posters of Amalfi and Positano on pine-clad walls; their eyes scrolled the right-hand side of the menu, settling for crêpes and coffee as they sighed into the empty spaces around them. She thinks now that she did all the sighing, while Bernie remained resolutely indifferent. Strange, she thinks, that her friend was the one who ended up married; it seems that all that indifference paid off in the long run. Moira looks towards the window and the figure of the man beyond.

Once, as fourteen- or fifteen-year-olds, they had ventured into the city at night. They dressed carefully, in their most grown-up clothes, with nylon stockings and shoes with raised heels, aware that the theatre where they were going was adult territory. They had heard mention of a play about a poet-patriot, from a teacher in school. They were in a romantic phase then, enraptured by the heroism of a life of poetry culminating in death for one's country. They each carried a commemorative coin, minted by the State, with the embossed side profile of the poet, allowing them a tactile encounter with their dead hero as he lay in their coat pockets. The fact that he was a flawed hero – the side-face pose that graced the coin and photos hid an eye defect – made him accessible for them even then, more than fifty years after his death. They never considered that his politics also might have been flawed.

The play had been everything that they had hoped for and they left the theatre elated. They walked carefully, stretching their young bodies upward in a stiff posture. The theatre-goers surged around them as they hastened towards home but the two girls were in no hurry. They chatted and laughed, frequently checking their reflections in shop windows as they passed. Voices swirled around them, loud then soft, fading into the distance. Behind them some young men were talking, persistently and close. The girls stopped talking and walked faster on their newly raised heels, tilting their chins in the belief that this might ward off any unwanted encounter

'Ah, wouldja look at them! Do their mammies know they're out?'

'Wouldja say they'd be up for it, or what?'

'You joking? Would ya look at the legs on them – like two pieces of straw hanging from a loft!'

Raucous laughter rose as the youths pushed and shoved around them, separating then regrouping, moving beyond them down the street, then vanishing into the throng. The two girls looked in shock and humiliation at each other, which slowly settled into something else. Bernie's eyes widened, then she guffawed, a coarse, snorting sound. Her friend stared at her, then she, too, started to laugh and they doubled up with mirth in the centre of the street, relief spilling around them as their sophistication evaporated into the night.

Moira longs to remind Bernie of this episode about their young selves, the thought of which still makes her laugh. She wants to hear her friend laugh too. But she thinks that it would become a story about two other people, unknown to Bernie, and in ways unknown to her too. There was always a hole in things, even then. The splitting chrysalis of their fourteen-year-old selves would remain invisible in the telling, and the emerging selfhood – a horrible word – the one that had collapsed in all that laughter, would be lost in the questioning and the probing, as Bernie attempted to make sense of it all.

She reaches into her bag and pulls out a handful of shells – for somehow Bernie constantly loses her shells – and scatters them before them. Worm-like lines of light emerge from beneath the shell holes and spread across the table, forming a web of radiance between them.

'Look, Bernie, these all have holes.'

Joan Leech

DOWN BY THE RIVERSIDE

Time was I woulda' clocked him one. Calling it 'a monstrosity'. He's so wrapped in his own happiness he can call it that.

You don't know I'm here. I'm safe here behind that stump of the tree I call his altar. I love to hide here for an hour, maybe more, every morning and talk to him, to the last place he was, and tell him I'm sorry, so sorry. If only I had the sense. I haven't seen anything else. From here I can see it all. Him an' his two kids and his make-believe blonde wife, all wellington-ed out for a walk by the river and it's not even raining.

Now I would say to him I just hope it keeps fine for you, son. I had a son. And in my heart, believe me, it's raining. And it'll be raining forever. This is all that I have left of him. Here on what you called a monstrosity now. Sense is costly.

Sometimes I get a smile, remembering ... that was his smelly little toy. He wouldn't let her wash it. Took it everywhere. None of us could put it in the bin. I nearly threw it into the river after him. But I couldn't. I can't let it go. All those things, his favourite mug, his football jersey. The holy things are there too. His Gran's beads, his First Communion photo. The smile on him and him missing a tooth. He was likely thinking about all the money. He was getting bolder and bolder according to his teachers. But they didn't know him. He was just not interested and wanted a laugh.

She saw him grow up and started to say stuff. I ignored it and probably opened another can. If he hadn't of learned to drink watchin' me at it he'd still be here. I haven't touched a drop since, nor will I.

'A dry drunk,' she calls me. Says I'm cross all the time an' that's why she's out every night of the week with her whist pals. And we're in separate rooms. I went into his room the first night and somehow stayed there.

The little fairy lights are funny and the batteries are with them. I s'pose the candles are no good on a windy night. He woulda' laughed at that. Was it his Gran left the angels and the holy pictures?

I just love sitting here where nobody can see me. An odd dog creeps up but after a smell, he leaves me be. Dogs don't like heartbreak.

If only the river wasn't so high that evenin'. One minute he's dancin' around to Thin Lizzy up on the bridge there, phone in one hand, can in the other, next he's shouting down the phone at her and the next he's in the river ... the guys are tryin' to make sense of what they're seeing ... they're down the slipway trying to reach him to pull him in. He never learned to swim. Neither did they, and anyway they were pissed. No lifebuoy. That's changed now. Too late for Matt.

They've all moved away. Even the one she married after. Cissy told me that. She was the one on the phone to him. Said she wanted to break it off because of his carry on. I see her pushing the pram and the bitta pink in the pram sleeping. She said to me it was all her fault at the funeral. She cried all the time. I told her it wasn't. I didn't tell her it was my fault but it was. I taught him to drink. Cissy said it must have been her who left the pink heart.

I wish Cissy would come down here an odd time with me. She only ever goes to the grave of a Sunday. It was good they found his soaked body but this is where he was last alive and I need that. Even when it rains – I love the feel of it. It's easier to cry in the rain. I tell him over and over I'm sorry.

'A big, sorry, sad monster,' she called me when she came in home last night. And now he calls the altar a 'monstrosity'.

Antoinette McCarthy

HISTRIONICS

We walk away. Away from the sunny side of the lake with the low stone wall, the cars and picnic benches.

The road, a horseshoe around the lake, rises slowly away from the water's edge on this side, trees filling the gap.

At a break in the wall we look down a steep muddy path through the forest, no light reaches here, last autumn's leaves here, but at the bottom a glimpse of silver shimmer shows that we can reach the lake.

'It will be easier on the way back up,' he says.

I slip my way down, the ground sliding under my feet.

There is a small cement jetty with deep steps down to the water.

We sit beside each other.

I pull out my cigarette tin, coax my trembling hands into the soft, delicate work of rolling. Everything feels tight, even my eyeballs. Light up. Deep pull twice. Nicotine and tar, arsenic and formaldehyde, sucked deep into my lungs. I am both poisoning and embalming myself at the same time. Always multitasking, me.

Pull, inhale, say nothing. Too soon for words.

It will be easier on the way back up. Fuck's sake.

The lake is still and smooth. A red buoy held motionless like a cake decoration sat into the icing.

A cluster of houses on the far bank. All the lights suddenly go on in one of them. A beacon. There she is, calling my attention. Her distress coming at me, skimming fast and low across the water.

'There's no privacy. Inside there's all of you. Outside we are literally in someone's back garden. I have no phone connection. I can't stay here. I need to go home NOW.'

We are on day two of our 'holiday'. First thing this morning I watched, from our glass-fronted cube, as our host family let the chickens out of their coop not twenty feet away. I hadn't even had a coffee yet when they trooped out in a line, like something from *Little House on the Prairie* in pyjamas.

I'm usually better at this, finding something with a bit of privacy, scanning for the gable end of the owner's property in the corner of the picture. Spotting the distortion you get from a wide-angled lens. But I feel addled, her adolescence is a constant gnawing thought like a rat keeping its teeth sharp. But sharp is not what I am. Dulled is what I am.

I root in the bag for my flask of water, I can't find it, the tin totters on my knee then falls.

'Oopsy daisy,' I say.

I must go back soon. The thought twitches away like a tic. I roll another fag. My mouth is dry.

I've been here before. Sitting, looking at the water, trying to pull myself together.

I slap my thigh, pantomime style. 'Right,' I say, and when I don't move, he looks at me.

'Right,' I say again and follow through this time, stand up.

I feel wobbly.

'You go first,' I say. 'I'm going to need help.'

He gets up and slowly moves ahead of me up the path.

I grab on to the back of his jacket. His good wool one he won't wear if it looks like rain.

When he feels the tug, he starts speaking softly: 'Not much further. Take your time. This is the worst bit.'

The light is fading fast. On the far side of the lake, car lights coil their way home.

I want to sit down but everywhere is damp and dark; the trees arch over the road making a tunnel. But there's light up ahead. Pick up the pace, it's like night in here. And there's that feeling of déjà vu again.

'Do you want me to carry your bag?' he says.

Jesus, I must look rough.

We step out into brightness, safer now but every step draws us closer to another dark tunnel.

She is waiting back in the holiday home. Angry, disillusioned, on the brink of despair. It makes me feel like a bullfighter, trying to avoid the horns of it all. Sidestepping her insistent demands once again.

I am in another dark tunnel and up ahead, in the distance, a patch of light. I've definitely been here before.

I'm looking around in my memory, looking for a little hand in mine, the rumble of a pushchair wheel. There is none. Before the children, then? I'm trying to find something to pull on.

Parking in the car, walking away from people until the road runs out. Sitting too long, staving off the dread of returning. Walking back through the dark and the light. And who were they then? The whirling dervish in the background that set my crazy going. Wind me up, ladies and gentlemen, and watch me spin. I find a thread, tug, up comes the tangle of sludge from the drain.

Someone as wide as they are tall looms in my mind, you know the shape, Old Queen Vic in her funeral weeds. Fixed bulk, a form of pure obstacle. My mother-in-law. That's who she was then. The one I had to armour myself against. Because now I come to think about it, forget the matador, think Tweedledum, pots and pans, that's what I've got.

And there it is.

That silhouette is not only a person, it's also a pot. My first visit to his family home. A huge stew pot, enough to feed a platoon. Just a pot of stew, but you didn't know her yet. It was strategic. Checkmate. Our inevitable ingratitude already stirred in.

As soon as we got inside, she was busying around it. Lifting the lid.

She turned. 'I was all day yesterday making it,' and a look of bitter disappointment on her face.

He muttered to me, 'She hates cooking. She is a very bad cook.'

She said, 'Will I heat the stew?'

Out of the corner of his mouth he said, 'She's trying it on because you're here. I haven't eaten her food in years and I'm not going to start now.'

He kept to that. The mood grew.

Enough stew to feed twelve people. It sat there for two days. The smell thinning out to stale, boiled bones. And every time we talked of food, lunch out or a takeaway, we would all look at it.

'Will I heat the stew?'

Every refusal brought her a step closer to the edge, until finally, she stomped off down the hall in a fit of despair and took to the bed.

In the morning the pot was gone. The stove top empty and wiped clean. I was relieved that this, our final day, would not be blighted by it. The visit could end on a good note. I made a cup of tea, went to get some milk. And there it was, the stew pot, filling every inch of her small fridge. She'd had to take the shelves out so that she could fit in the lid.

The first was my mother-in-law and now my daughter.

'I can't stay here. I have no privacy. I haven't slept. I can hear Dad snoring. I can hear you breathing. I'll hitch. I'll walk until I find a bus. I'm leaving whether you like it or not.'

'Will I heat the stew?'

Twenty years later and I am on the same road, looking out at the light from the dark, trying to arm myself against the onslaught. Not knowing now, as I didn't know then, whether I can do this. Whether this will be the moment when it will be all too much.

There are people up ahead. They're coming out from the dark. Two men, one who wears sunglasses, the other, who walks slightly behind, stays in the shadows. We passed before on the way out, but we pretend we haven't. Go through the same script.

'It's a grand evening.'

'It is, thank God.'

I am so convincing, such an illusion of solidity. They have no idea that I might fall apart here. Drop to the ground and bits of me will roll away, an arm trundling down the hill while my head is away down the road.

But it's alright, though. My belittling of my peril is starting to take hold. I can feel it. Denial is setting in. I over-dramatise, you know.

'It's like I'm going home to face my mum,' he says.

I look at him, this man who walked beside me then and walks beside me still.

'It's funny you should say that,' I say. 'We have in fact been here before.'

We break cover, the trees behind us. At last we're out in the open.

I stop and lean over the wall to look down into the lake below. Take a deep breath. There is a large grey fish moving around down there. Now I've seen two others appear, from out behind rocks and under seaweed they swim, hoovering along the bottom with open, fleshy mouths.

A couple walks towards us. The woman stops and leans over the wall to see what I'm looking at.

'Look at that huge fish,' she says.

And leans further still, out over the wall, to track its path. There's a cry. She has tipped too far. She flails her arms around like something from a silent movie. As if she's about to fall in.

The man leaps forward and pulls her back, wrapping his arms around her, holding her tight.

'I really thought I was a goner there,' she says.

And she looks up at him shocked but grateful, like she's just had the fright of her life.

I want to say, 'Ah here now, Missus, enough of the theatrics, we all know you weren't going anywhere.'

But I keep my mouth shut and carry on walking.

Ann McKay

NORTHERN PRIMAVERA

The fingers of the hands of the branches
of the evergreens comb her passing.

      Ever alert, the birds shout out about her advent,
               wings and tails tingling.

Perfumes – resinous, mouldy, dank,
emergent green – scent her breathing air.

      Moss-trees, pine needles, beech mast, humus,
    rabbit-pills, down-wisps from wood-pigeons' bellies,
        bright quartz chippings, dark bog muck –
      all give as they take her light and heavy steps.

The print and track of her passing
touch with firm pressure roots and shoots below –
they stir, like deep-sleeping babies waking up.

      Ladybirds, slaters, clocks and caterpillars,
    millipedes, midges, moths and worms and grubs
    and ants bestir themselves, quicken to the chill,
          the dabs of warmth.

Cows and sheep sense movement in their wombs,
a tickle of a trickle of a flow in their teats.

      Grey air harassing hills backs off,
    shows hints of other colours it can wear,
    blue fleetingly, its fleshy pinks flirtatious.

The word is out. She's here.
Her alto-cirrus face and hair.
She's here again. Her sedimentary feet.
She's here. Here she is –
Brigit.

> Brigit, give us a spring in our heels.
> Give us buds and eggs and truer words and sap.
> White as snowdrops, let our ink-of-milk flow.
> Let sparks fly when we speak.

Give us the germ of an idea, to bake the bread with,
to begin to live on.
Give us a spring to heal the here and the now,
Brigit. Here. Now.

> We're awake, awaiting it –
> the heart-felt imprint of your poised foot's fall.

Marilyn McLaughlin

THINGS HEARD

in the early-morning, nearly-empty coffee shop:
the brisk clatter of cups, the click of high heels,
the steady burr of machinery, cooling, heating.
Milk and sugar in your Americano? That's you now.

The brisk clatter of cups, the click of high heels,
the whisper of a girl's coat on a chair at the next table.
Milk and sugar in your Americano? That's you now.
A whoosh as the door opens, the snore of a passing bus.

The whisper of a girl's coat on a chair at the next table
where the man she's with allows long silences to grow.
A whoosh as the door opens, the snore of a passing bus.
She says: *What I'd really like is to be fluent.*

The man she's with allows long silences to grow.
I'm close to that, tantalisingly close to that,
she says. *What I'd really like is to be fluent.*
Nearby, old neighbours tally the quick and the dead.

I'm close to that, tantalisingly close to that.
Someone leaves, the door bounces lightly behind him.
Nearby, old neighbours tally the quick and the dead.
Traffic sounds like the wash of waves on a far shore.

Someone leaves, the door bounces lightly behind him.
Beyond the steady burr of machinery cooling, heating,
traffic sounds like the wash of waves on a far shore
in the early-morning, nearly-empty coffee shop.

Gift for a New Baby

Her feet, kicking at air,
still know the gist of flight
from tethered liquid days
afloat — tiny astronaut
space walking. She has not yet
unlearned weightlessness.

Birds do not surprise her —
toss of garden sparrows,
gale-riding gulls, nor clouds,
or aeroplanes, the floating
moon, balloons on strings,
litter aloft on the wind.

I buy her red velvet shoes
with satin bows and buttoned
straps, third size, six months
to a year. By then she'll be
well launched on the long
negotiation with gravity.

I HAD RED SHOES ONCE

When I stopped being a hippy
I bought red shoes – platforms,
stacked heels, buckled ankle straps.
I wore them every day, teetering
off to class and coffee across
Front Square. I brought them home,
left them in Pollocks Shoe Shop
on the Strand Road for repair.

No other shoes stomped and clumped
in such a satisfactory way and they
made me tall. But before I got them back
they were blown up, by those who loved
Ireland but not Pollocks Shoe Shop,
where I'd stood in the X-ray machine
every year to check the fit of sensible
brown shoes for school and Sundays.

Three minutes to get out, *tick, tick, tick.*
The shoes were all too slow – flew
through the roof: brogues, court shoes,
old ladies' shoes, shoe-horns and laces
all trying out the air. And then they fell,
a silent snowfall of slippers, a patter
of baby shoes, a tapping of stilettos
sharp as hailstones on the pavement.

But my unsuitable red shoes tap-danced
along the ridge pole of the bank next door
glissaded down the Bangor Blue slates of its roof,
leapt like a defecting Russian ballet dancer, clean over
the Strand Road – dizzying enjambement – They were
last seen River-Dancing off towards the quays,
looking to jump ship.

Liz McManus

SOVIET (*extract*)

Staff at Monaghan Lunatic Asylum Declare Soviet Rule
On 29 January 1919 fifty-two male attendants and forty-two
female nurses occupied the main buildings of their workplace.
The workers made Donegal-native Peadar O'Donnell their
leader and for almost a week they ran the institution under
O'Donnell's instruction ... [T]he workers, fearing some sort of
conflict, armed themselves with sticks and iron bars ... They
also dressed in the inmates' uniforms to create confusion.
                                    – *Irish Independent,* January 1919

I enjoyed looking, through the keyhole, at the nurses as
they passed in the corridor and the inmates carrying their
bundles to the laundry. Most of the time there was nothing
to see. I looked out the window too, but that was hard on
my legs. I had to stand on my tiptoes. Sometimes, through
the window, I saw a herd of goats in the field and the boy,
Jimmy, minding them. Around me, in the dormitory, the
racket made by the women was unbearable: the old crone
in the bed singing hymns and the women screeching like
cats until the nurse came in and separated them. Then we

were led down, two by two, to the dining hall. I always sat in a corner, quiet as a mouse. Even then, the noise hurt my ears.

I looked out so that I could breathe.

Everything changed when the Soviet began. That morning the nurse led us out of the dormitory as usual. Then she said, 'You are free to go wherever you like.'

I couldn't believe it. I ran upstairs, thinking they'd come after me and lock me away but no one did. The upper corridor was similar to the one I had left, with closed doors on either side. When I saw a ladder leading up to a trap door in the roof, my skin prickled.

No one will find me there ...

The attic was warm and bright with five dormer windows. I lay down among the old crates and boxes, and gloried in the silence. It was a gift from God: the peace was broken by the sound of birds chattering and, in the eaves, the wind's moan. I didn't want to remember, but memories, uninvited, crowded in. *It's only a baby,* my mother told me after she had taken it away and thrown it in the river. I was twelve years of age at the time, I think. My father beat me when he found me wading into the river in search of the poor wee mite. If I keep looking, I told him, the baby will fly up like an angel out of the water and settle in my hands. But he wouldn't listen. The next day he brought me here, to the Mental in Monaghan town, and left me at the gate. I haven't seen my father or my mother since.

When I heard the creak of the ladder I was so frightened I jumped up, yelling, 'Go away!'

A man's voice. 'What have we here?'

I could tell from his uniform that he was an attendant and I could tell too, by the way he took my hand, that he would do me no harm.

'Will you help me raise the flag?'

What?

Then I saw the flag in his hand: a rich crimson unfurling.

'Hold you that end,' he said, 'while I fix the other.'

After we hung the flag out the window, it surged like something alive. The man smiled. 'Downstairs with you now.'

The dining hall was teeming with men and women: attendants, nurses, inmates. A man I had never seen before was standing up on a table. He said that a Soviet had been established and everyone cheered. I thought he was sending us out into the fields to sow seeds or that he wanted us to sew sheets in the laundry. I could see the attendants running around barricading the windows and doors. *To keep the polis out* ... and everyone cheered again.

'A Soviet, what does that mean?' I asked the nurse who held the key to our dormitory. She had her arms around an attendant's neck and the two of them were jumping around like children. 'It means we will get our rightful pay and rightful hours at last.'

On the second day, the polis arrived but they left us alone. They bedded down on straw in the recreation room while we slept in our beds. The stranger directed lookouts to keep watch just in case the polis tried to break through the barricades. In the dining hall the men were instructed to exchange their uniforms with the attendants and the women with the nurses. That left me: I was so small in stature the only one I could exchange my dress with was the boy, Jimmy. I didn't like the goaty smell of his old trousers but when I saw him in my dress I laughed out loud. He got angry and flounced away from me, just like a girl would.

Well, I thought, I will be the boy then, and tend to the goats. To touch their skinny backs and tickle them under their whiskery chins, I wanted that more than anything. It was a dream I had: to wander out in the fields, to lie down in the green grass and smell the earth beneath my body. Oh yes. But there was no way out. Every door had been barricaded and every window was locked. I sat down in the corridor and waited, without knowing why. For a door to open, maybe?

When evening fell, the lamps were lit and tea, bread and butter was set out in the dining hall, just like any other day, except we heard music coming from the recreation room.

After our supper was over, the Donegal stranger said, 'Since the polis are having a hooley, so will we.'

And the men pushed back the tables and forms and cleared a space for dancing. Old mad Malachy took out his fiddle. I don't know why he was the only inmate who was called mad. Weren't we all supposed to be?

As I watched the dancers fill the room, the sound of the music flooded through me. Oh, how I loved those reels, jigs and polkas. And Jimmy was out on the floor with the best of them. Something gave way inside me when the music started and I saw that boy dance. The way he slipped between the dancers, spinning around, the folds of my dress opening like petals, his bare feet so light on the floor they hardly touched the boards. He was so beautiful, his scraggy hair turned gold by the sun, that I was filled with wonder. On that night, everything was different: attendants danced with inmates, nurses with other nurses.

It was hard to tell one from the other. It seemed to me that we had all shed ourselves along with our uniforms and taken on a new way of being. Each one had been set free by the strange circumstances that we were in.

One of the dancers was an angel, and he was wearing my dress. *Jimmy,* I cried out but I couldn't find him in the swirl of people, as if he had flown up through the roof of the dining hall and left me behind on the ground.

My memories came crowding in again: I was in the river's flow, searching for the part of me that had been swept away. *It's only a baby* ... my mother said and my father was standing in the light of the window, as black as the Devil.

By the fourth day the polismen had got weary of sleeping on straw and they went away. We watched them through the windows and laughed. 'Cowards,' I heard one inmate say, 'we could have trounced them,' but he was only blackguarding. All we had to fight with was shovels and pitchforks, while the polis had guns.

Once they were gone, we reclaimed the recreation room and the Donegal stranger stood up on a table and gave a speech. He spoke about emancipation ... capitalism ... the working class. I could tell from the expressions around me that I wasn't the only one who was bewildered.

Then he said something we all understood: 'We must remain in here until we win. That is our last word.'

When he said that, everyone clapped loudly. O'Donnell Abú they called him. He was our leader. And sure enough, it wasn't long before the first offer came in from the Asylum Committee. There was a big increase in pay to be given to the men and a lesser increase for the women. When they heard about the offer, the nurses were fit to be tied. As they marched along the corridor towards the

Donegal stranger's room you could hear them roaring, 'We want equal pay and that is our last word!'

And O'Donnell Abú agreed with them.

'Aye,' he said, 'we will sit it out and wait for a better offer.'

It took three more days, and when the better offer came, everyone cheered. The nurses had won. The Soviet was over. The Mental went back to its old ways. Jimmy and I took in the red flag from the attic window. After we exchanged our clothes again, his goaty smell lingered on my dress for days.

Now, when I look out the dormitory window, I can see Jimmy minding the goats. He looks shrunken in his dirty moleskin trousers and torn shirt. His hair is thinner. I think he is going bald.

There was a time when a goatherd danced like an angel but it seems a long time ago. I don't wish to look back. These days, I prefer to spend my time looking through the keyhole.

When I was sixteen, my mother came and took me away from the Mental. That was the time I felt the roughness of her hand in mine and her breath on my cheek.

'Sling off your boots,' she said, and the two of us walked out along the road in our bare feet and our boots hanging off our shoulders. Grey clouds hung heavy on grey fields. Then the clouds cleared. It was like a dream: on that May morning, the two of us walking side by side and talking.

'I hear they had you working on a farm,' my mother said.

Yes, I was so proud of myself. 'Last year they had us out snagging turnips. I was the best of them all, the farmer said. Thon doddering women were no match for me.'

As I spoke, my mother listened, her eyes narrow and crinkled. 'That so?' she said, nodding her head, 'That so?' I was so happy that I wanted the two of us to keep walking as far as the other side of Ireland and beyond, but when we came into the town, my mother sat down on the footpath and put on her boots and told me to do the same.

'It's time you went to work, daughter.'

There was such noise I wasn't sure if I heard her right. Crowds of people were milling around us: young girls and boys carrying parcels under their oxters and fat old farmers standing apart, with sticks in their hands like they were about to drive their cattle out. One farmer came up to my mother and nodded. Then he looked me up and down.

'Are you for hiring, wee girl?'

'She is,' my mother said.

'Can she milk a cow, can she wash, cook and churn?'

'Aye, she can.'

I pulled on my mother's sleeve but she paid no heed.

'Five pound and no more.'

My mother laughed, 'Are you joking me?'

'Five pound and two shillings and no more, I said.'

And so it went on until they agreed a price and he put money in her hand for an earl and they both spat on it.

'Meet me at four o'clock outside the tea shop,' the farmer said to me and I didn't say a word. What did he want with me, that old, smelly farmer? My mother was busy pocketing the coin and straightening up her coat to leave. I knew then that she intended to go on without me and I was frightened at the thought.

'Mammy,' I cried, 'I don't know how to milk a cow.'

But she had folded herself into the crowd and disappeared, her words in my ears: 'I will see you at the next fair day, daughter.'

It didn't take the farmer long to discover that I couldn't do any of things he wanted me to do. Milking the cows was easy once I knew how but I couldn't cook to save my life. One day I dropped the milk jug and it broke in smithereens on the floor. The farmer took up his stick to beat me but he slipped on the puddle of milk and landed on his backside, roaring. In the middle of it all, his son came into the kitchen and when he saw me standing there, with the stick over my head and his father stretched out, boking with fright, he laughed so hard that I began to laugh too.

The son's name was Tom. Tom McShane. He began watching me when I was at my chores. He had a curious look on his face. I didn't mind. It gave me some kind of power over him. *Take off your boots in the house*, I'd say to him. *Bring in the turf*. Often when I went to the cow byre, he followed me like a lamb after its mother, and once I had milked the cows, I let him lie down with me in the straw. Afterward he never said a word but, at other times, if I displeased him, he took his stick to me. His ways were unfathomable: at one time so gentle and loving and at another there was a mad rage in his head.

Each month I sent money to my mother. When the six months were up, I went to meet her in the town. This time, I thought, she will bring me home at last. I dreaded the thought of meeting my father but I was not afraid of him anymore. I was a grown woman now and I knew my own strength. Although on one important matter I was still ignorant.

As soon as she saw me, my mother knew what Tom McShane had done and she marched me back to the old farmer who was minding his own business, having a quiet pint in Duffy's public house on the Square.

The bar was empty apart from him and three men standing at the counter. When my mother burst through the door they turned around quick.

'Are you the father?'

Old farmer McShane looked dumbstruck. The men at the bar laughed,

'Fair play, old man,' one man said.

'Go on,' said another. 'Shame the Devil.'

For a second time, the farmer and my mother began to haggle over me, just as they had done at the fair in May. He called her every name under the sun but to no avail. When she threatened to go to the priest he caved in. They spat on their hands and agreed: Tom and I were to marry and no more money would be sent to my mother.

From then on, I worked as hard as I ever did but, once we were wed, there was a place for me in Tom's bed and at the table where we ate. Old man McShane lived long enough to hold his first grandson in his arms, although he didn't seem bothered about it, one way or the other. In the following winter he failed fast and by the new year he was stretched out in his coffin. Then it was just my husband, me and the baby and another one on the way. I had hoped that marriage might change Tom, soften him in some way, but he remained the same: a gentle soul at times, and, at other times, when he had drink taken, as cruel a man as was ever born.

It was a lonely house where we lived: out on the hillside, with no neighbour nearby, bar one: a Protestant woman who lived at the next farm. Mrs McNair kept herself to herself. I hardly ever saw her, for she had an ailing husband and she didn't go to Mass.

Once, when I was walking back from the town of Clones carrying a load of nails and baling twine, the handle of my basket broke and the nails spilled out. I took the baby out from inside my shawl and placed him on the rushy bank beside the road. I was so busy searching for nails in the mud that I didn't hear the horse and cart coming.

When I looked up, the horse had stopped and a woman was climbing down off the cart. My neighbour. Up close Mrs McNair was a big bony woman, with eyes as pale as forget-me-nots. I bowed my head but not before I saw a smile flit across her face.

'Is that the baby Moses amid the bulrushes?'

I didn't know what she was talking about but it didn't matter. She knelt down in the mud to help me. When she stood up Mrs McNair didn't seem to care that her skirts were marked by two muddy knee-stains. One last nail was missing. She lifted her boot: there it was, in the mud, the head of it winking. What Tom would have done if I had lost a nail didn't bear thinking about.

'Lift you up thon wean,' Mrs McNair said, 'and I will bring you home.'

Lia Mills

THE WOOING OF EMER
An old story, retold

My bad leg aches. It drags a little when I'm tired. Cullen
liked it, said the limp gave me the look of a creature
getting ready to leap in two directions at once. He was a
great one for the leaping: no wall high enough to keep him
out, no horse fast enough to outrun him.

There was a night he stood behind me at the sink when I
was doing the dishes, up to my elbows in soapy water. The
wall he was. I leaned back and back and he was still there
under me, lifting me, bubbles floating off, a small world in
each and every one of them. *Pop!* – another one gone, and
Cullen still there. What else could I do? I knew nothing
outside this place, only the ones that came and the ones
that went, and he was the best of them. Back in the
glorious, the gory, days. Depends who you talk to, now,
was he hero or villain.

A full-throated roar, like an army on the move or a
sports crowd, sounded way off in the distance, long before

Cullen's flash Lotus turned into our lane that first time, someone else driving. That way he could move as fast as he liked; someone else's licence to be lost – not that I saw that then.

The first time I saw him I felt a tug at the root, an entanglement, deep and low, when he'd done no more than take my hand and say hello. He was tall, solid, more weathered than he should be. Once my eyes locked with his I couldn't look away, his pupils a bottomless black. There seemed to be more of them than there should, but when I looked harder there were only the two. I'd never seen the like before, watched him to see would I catch it again. He caught me looking. Our father was away that time but Cullen let me know, without saying as much in anyone else's hearing, that he'd come for me. My stepmother made him stay for dinner. It was the code of the house, no one could leave unfed.

Strange meanings hid inside his words. He mentioned places I wanted to see, weird transactions, old wrongs. Firelight sparked in his nut-brown hair. Shadows moved on the walls. I worked my hooked silver needle. A shawl flowered from my fingers while my questions drew him out. Phrases flowed between us as though poured from a crystal jug. The room was full of people who heard nothing out of the ordinary, but our every syllable was charged enough to power a small town.

I said I was as good as a prisoner, the way my every move was watched. It was as well my father was away, strange that no one had come to interrupt us. He said he'd kill for me if he had to, all I had to do was say the word. 'And what word would that be?' I asked, fool that I was, mocking. 'You'd have some battle on your hands.'

I swear he got bigger. His spine lengthened; his ribs lifted. Extra shadows in his eyes. 'Do you know who you're talking to, girl?'

And he the same age as me.

He carried himself like an older man but was vain as a marriageable girl. He'd a softening effect on women, it worked overtime on me. I spoke nonsense to him that day, not knowing what I was dealing with. 'You wouldn't have to kill everyone,' I said. 'There's the bodyguards and the drivers, I'd want rid of those alright, but you'd spare my brothers. I wouldn't want them on my conscience.'

He said we were a match; he'd never met a woman yet who could keep up with him for talk. He admired my skill with a needle, said it was close to magic, to spin cloaks from a hooked needle, to weave threads and bind seams so close together the stitching was invisible and no one could pull them apart. 'You and I could be like that.'

'I don't know you.'

He reared up. 'Where I come from, everyone knows me.'

I rolled my shoulders. 'We haven't heard of you here.'

He broke the look we'd been holding uncomfortably long to gaze at the base of my throat, then lower.

I covered the place where the yoke of my dress met bare skin with the flat of my hand. I'd good hands. Long fingers. 'There'll be none of that,' I said. 'I know nothing about you, only what you say. Besides, I'm watched every second. There are eyes on us now. That's one of our drivers over there, talking to my stepmother. His back is turned, but see the way he's looking, through that mirror, there? There's another at the foot of the stairs, pretending to read his phone.'

My sister, Dana, sat coiled into a chair near the fire, twisting a lock of pure gold hair on a spindle of finger, watching our foster-sister, Orla, play with a kitten. As though she felt my look, she stirred and looked over at me, then at Cullen, then away again with a little shake of her bright head.

I plunged on, sheep as lamb. 'You might want to watch yourself, leaving. If my father and brothers were here, you'd not have got through the gates. You'll have that pair over there to deal with on your way out and remember, there's cameras everywhere.'

When it came to it, I walked him to his car. Orla came with. Our stepmother and Dana stood in the spill of light on the steps, watching; two guards on the inner gate.

Back inside, Dana said, 'I never met a man so fond of the sound of his own voice.'

Our stepmother circled my wrist with her fingers, pressing the small blue thread that pulses there. She kept her eyes on me. 'He's long-winded alright.'

'His manners.' Dana wrinkled her neat little nose. 'The clothes. Crumpled, like he'd been wearing them for days.'

His clothes didn't interest me. Why would they, when I could see for myself the width of his shoulders, his sturdy thighs, the span of his hands? I pulled away from them, faked a yawn. 'Long day. I'm off to bed.'

It was summer, all the windows wide open. That night, when my sheets wound around my body, I felt, not cotton against my skin but muscle, sinew, bone.

He came and went, went and came. After that first encounter he didn't talk much. When he did he talked prices: cattle. Sheep. Vodka and cigarettes. He left tales of his escapades to others. He worked for a powerful man, in the business of moving consignments across the border – the border itself not a thing he cared to acknowledge, having been born in that region. He brought gifts. Stockings and linen for my stepmother and sisters, a yellow songbird in a cage for me, butter for the table, whiskey for my father. I never asked what business they had with each other and they never said what it was that my father sent north or what he got in return. They weren't accountable men.

I could feel Cullen's eyes on me, even through doors. Even in the dark.

The first time he asked for my hand, my father said no, he'd bring nothing but grief. 'Ulstermen are tricky and that one's trickier than most. There's trouble brewing up there,' he said.

Cullen came to say goodbye. He found me at the sink again, running the hot tap. I felt his bulk behind me, like something I'd always known. The steam made my eyes weak. Staring into the soap's scummy froth I felt myself dissolve, the future a place under water I was falling into. He caught me around the waist. *Whoa.* He could have been talking to a horse. This time I turned to lean against him. He smelled of autumn leaves and smoky fires, of something pearled and underground, yeasty. He said he intended to marry me, what did I think of that? I stood back a little then, to see what his eyes were doing. 'Dana is older,' I said. 'She should marry first. Would you not want her instead? Most men would.' He said word was that some men already had. He'd no interest in that kind of woman. I shivered, looked down at my feet. They seemed a long way away. His arms made a wall around me, tightening. He asked again.

I said I would, into his neck. He didn't hear. I had to lift my head and look into his broad freckled face and say yes again, fighting to stay awake under the spell of those marbled eyes of his, their flecks of fire, the dark tunnels that came and went in their shadows. He said to wait, that he'd be back, come hell or flood, when he'd learned a better trade, more to my father's liking.

That was put down to me, later. They said I made him go, out of vanity. Or pride. I suppose I was proud – what young person isn't? Is it wrong to want the best? But it wasn't me who sent him away. It was my father played a trick, dropping in on Cullen's boss in the North, going on about the online world, cyber training, the dark web, new kinds of security. Changing times. And wasn't Cullen – the coming man, star in the making, already a champion – the very one to send away to learn the skills of the future, even if it meant going so far away and for so long a time, to countries the likes of us never visited? Places you had to play tricks to get into and those you'd be lucky to leave alive. Layers upon layers of protection to penetrate, codes to learn and passwords, incomprehensible languages with strange, ever-changing lettering. Worlds within worlds but outside time. Cullen would have to use his wits to cross *those* borders, but wasn't he well up to it, weren't borders his particular thing?

I knew well what my father was at, black-hearted bastard that he was. I tried to warn Cullen before he left but he was already away in his head, thinking about the tests he'd been specially chosen for. 'That was my father put the idea in your Boss's head,' I told him. 'He thinks if you go far enough away, you'll get lost, or killed. Or find another woman, one you'd like better.'

He said he wasn't one to heed a warning or avoid a challenge, as I should know by now. As for another woman, he swore he wouldn't lie with anyone 'til he'd come back for me. He made me swear the same, that way we'd be all the sweeter for each other when our time came, for waiting.

Long years he was gone. I taught myself patience, stitched a trousseau and dreamed about when I'd leave Ticknock, my father's house, with him and go out into the wide world.

There were rumours. A woman, a child. A different woman. When he came back, my father said *No!* and *Get out of my house. Let me never see you again.* He'd heard those stories too.

Cullen laughed, put his arm around me, right there in front of them all. 'Will you?' he said in my ear.

'I will.'

'Wait here for me, so.'

I sat in the dark and watched for him. One minute the house was alive with people: footsteps, voices and banging doors. Then they were all asleep. I never asked how he did it. Something in the wine he'd warned me not to drink? What matter? He came in the night and lifted the front door, whole and entire, from its hinges, like the lid of a coffin, left it lying on the gravel like some dead, useless beast. We walked out and onto the road, where the Lotus was hidden in the hedge. No sign of his driver. Nor mine, come to that.

'You were sure of yourself,' I said.

'I wasn't wrong.'

His voice hummed in my own throat, sent echoes deep inside my lungs, under my heart, where my own voice came from. No, he wasn't wrong.

Not right either. Oh, there was deliciousness alright. I was like a cat, a single touch enough to set me purring, rolling up to a boil in no time flat. A glance from him could melt stone, he was known for it. Imagine what it could do to me, besotted as I was. But after a time of traipsing from boarding house to boarding house, putting up with the whims and moods of landladies, while he came and went exactly as he had before, handling security for the Boss in every county in Ireland, I'd had enough of damp sheets, narrow creaking beds, dirty windows, recycled teabags, other people's smells. What had seemed a life of adventure to me, the world wide open before us, was a pattern ingrained in him, little room for me in it. He couldn't stay still long enough to find a decent place to live. What of it, he'd say, when he knew places we could stop overnight or for a week, no questions asked. He'd have slept standing up if he could. Like a horse. There were those who called him Dog, for his loyalty to the Boss and the boss before that one. Sometimes the people he visited would put us up for the night, but that was nearly worse. Small talk, opinions, attempts to make me talk about the Boss's people, ones I barely knew. My life was a state of fragmented, uneasy boredom. Like a boat on many choppy, unsettling waters. Then I fell pregnant.

If you're going to raise a child you need somewhere to do it. It could be any place, but I longed for home. As soon as my head hit the pillow at night, Ticknock rose from the dark of whatever temporary rooms we happened to be in, to pull me back. No longer a well, I was all river, craving sea.

A crow came to my window and knocked on the glass. That settled it, I had to go home. At the very least I'd have my baby there.

Clodagh was an equinox baby, born on the cusp of autumn, ushering in a season of gales and storms, high tides, rain, floods and broken power lines. Trees snapped in half, their creamy innards wrenched out and exposed to rain. The sharp stink of resin clung to everything. Leaves blew like vivid snow across the sky, scarlet gold flocks tumbled to earth, piled high in gutters and clung to the wheel rims of cars.

I relished it all, an excuse to stay indoors, curled up with my baby in the high bed I'd been born in. My parents were abroad. The weather kept everyone away except the community nurse and the deliverymen who brought coal and groceries. My husband already gone back to his shady business in the border counties. I should have remembered, a man who'll turn his back on one child will think nothing of doing it again.

Such thoughts were far from me then. Lying on in bed with Clodagh through bitter winter mornings, I dreamed of spring, of pale flowers and air warm and soft as milk to counteract the dark ferocity of my daughter, whose thick eyebrows met in the middle, who had a pelt of dark hair from shoulders to waist. Her cry was imperious, even then. Far from the helpless infant I'd been warned to expect, she was loud, vigorous. She bullied me from the beginning.

We stayed in Ticknock as long as we decently could. My parents came home from their winter abroad and said I knew where my place was, no one to blame but myself. So I brought the baby north to Cullen's place of work and they gave us a house to live in. Cullen carried on his old ways, exactly as he had before. I was the one who changed. I'd discovered strengths of my own.

Despite my childish dream of free movement through a wide-open world I was glad of my own walls and their door. It wasn't unlike being in Ticknock: cameras everywhere, beyond the estate and within it. I was glad of the company of women, even if they teased me about breaking their hearts. To a girl, they'd fancied Cullen rotten when they were younger. Sympathy in some eyes, and questions. He was a short-fused man, no doubt about it. So things went on for a while. Two years to the day after Clodagh, Donal arrived, stocky, his fat lower lip already set in a pout. A mistake I'd pay for – Clodagh was the sort of child who could never get enough attention. It was far too soon for her to have to share me with anything so dull and unrewarding as another baby.

Everything changes when you have children. Everything. When you go into that fiery tunnel, no one tells you that the creature who comes out the far side of it will not be you. You will be both less and more than you were before. Less than you have ever imagined yourself to be, more because you're part of something different, a different way of being in the world. You have both split and merged. Those fractures will continue, every time more so. No wonder we look back and wonder what we've lost along the way.

Gadding about the place is all very well when you've no one only yourselves to think of, entranced by days of love and their astonishing nights. A child brings all that crashing to an end. She throws up barriers of sound. Stunned, sleepless, you hardly know if day is giving way to night or is night reversing into days you could swear you've already lived and left behind – days just like this one, like the ones that came before and those that will be next, and you see no end to it.

So the first thing is that you no longer have energy for gallivanting, even if it didn't suddenly take years to cross a threshold, your hands no longer free, burdens swinging from your arms, your breasts; eyes calling yours away from the open door.

And still Cullen came and went as he pleased. Came and went, went and came, as he had before and always there were women in love with him, women in thrall to him, women he was taken with himself. Never mind, my friends said. You're the one that matters, you're the one he married, you have his children.

Get over it.

I'd known he was unusual when I chose him and he chose me, full of energy and strength that needed channelling. My stepmother said, *Don't say we didn't warn you* and *You've made your bed.* My sister Dana said, *What did you expect?* So I stayed put and I have to admit it wasn't all bad. But something turned the air around us sour.

Stories followed him, clung to him and grew. You wouldn't know what to believe. A boy turned up, looking for his father. I'd have let him stay, but Cullen would have none of it. He set up a series of tests to make the boy prove himself. That boy died, unclaimed, trying to impress his own father.

You can't think the same of someone after that.

My own father died. Months later, a letter came from Orla. My stepmother was not herself. Ticknock falling into disrepair: a cracked window at the front, the garden overgrown.

That morning started out like any other when Cullen was getting ready to leave on business I'd rather not know about. This time, he'd be gone for months. He was at the table, quiet, his bag at the door. A driver due any minute. Once he'd have bored me with every twist and turn of last night's dreams. I'd puzzle them out for clues – not to his future, but to the workings of his mind. We were long past all that by the day in question. Silence was easier. I could read anything into it. Comfort. Worry. Barbs and spikes. My marriage a story I told in my head, a game plan, while he went about his business and I mine. Friendly, mind. Civil – I saw to that. There were the children to consider.

Crossing the room with a plate of toast that morning, I was struck by the column of his neck, the collar of his shirt a noose around it. The spread of his shoulders as wide a surface as an assassin could hope for. I opened my mouth to say *Stay* but no sound came out. He was peeling a hangnail. 'I'm in a hurry,' he said. I put the plate down in front of him and remarked on the weather, the likely condition of the roads. We were easy enough when we had to be.

A knock at the door. Orla's letter.

'What is it?' he asked.

'My stepmother needs help.' I looked into his broad freckled face and saw a stranger. 'I'll take the children and go to her.'

'How long?'

My eyes went to his hands. 'As long as it takes. You'd know where we are.'

He spread his fingers on the table and pushed himself back to stand. Fingertips the shape of spades. 'I'll be off, so.'

I knew I wouldn't see him again. One day, someone would come to my door and say he'd been found, face-down in an alley, a knife in his back; or broken at the bottom of a well; tied to a lamp post. What matter? It would be rough. Ugly. Bloody. He wouldn't go easy. Whatever was coming would come. When I looked into the future, as I sometimes could, a thing I never saw was Cullen an old man.

Research conducted while writing The Wooing of Emer *was funded by the Irish Research Council under grant number GOIPG/2020/349.*

Sara Mullen

Vault

In art class
we started with ellipses,
curves pencilled
haltingly around axes
to create not space
but solid-looking discs
set stiffly atop
flowerpots,
saucers, cups.

This perfect one,
a stilled meniscus,
draws on the entrails
past tipping point.
It whispers,
pull the floor up
till you can touch it
almost, no chasm here
at all, just jump.

SKRY

Juddering view,
dank embankments.
Halftone day gives way
to noirs of nightfall.

Your book left down,
a fellow passenger
bids to pick it up.
In window glass

you watch her
reflection: luminous,
lost in pages of pastels,
liminal flickerings

kindling her face
awake in gold,
glancing florals and
polychromatic votives.

This book, she says
returning it, my call
back to colour, to dust off,
take up my chalks again.

Your stop reels up.
You wish her well,
step out into the black
of hatched galaxies.

FRY PLACE

You let yourself
in at night, walk
the old rooms

all soft with
carpets and
wallpaper

layers damping
the sounds of
the town outside.

Turf burning
slow and rosy
in the hearths,

the sideboards
stacked with
tasselled boxes

filled with
whispers and
mysteries; the

square kitchen,
its clear floor
a chequerboard;

a tabby cat
squirrelled
in the nook

high above
the oven.
Door open

to the night, the
yard candlelit
as if awaiting

a party
of ghosts
yet to gather.

Stirrings
on the stairs;
one evening

you'll wait on the
bottom step for
someone to appear.

Patsy J. Murphy

A CHILD IN RATHMINES (*extract*)

Dublin 1948, Julia Prepares for England

The following morning, Julia and her grandfather took the tram to O'Connell Street and then walked along the quays towards Kingsbridge. Julia liked to dawdle and look at the old books, watch the flower seller and the men in bowler hats hurrying into dark offices. She especially loved looking up at the building on the corner of Parliament Street and Essex Quay with its tiles of blue showing a white donkey pulling a cart. Ladies in long dresses worked at a washtub, while the men struggled under heavy loads of clothes, and naked children played around them.

'Why were some men building an arch, and why was there a stove in the pictures?' she had asked Grandpan, but he had said the decorations around the building were telling the story of soap. Julia thought it must be about something more interesting than soap.

Grandpan's friend and old neighbour from Cullendaly had his tailor's rooms on the second floor of a rickety building a few doors down Essex Quay. You climbed up very steep dark stairs, passing a watchmaker and a solicitor's office on the way. The dank, foggy smell off the Liffey surrounded you as you climbed the stairs. The only way to see was through the light creeping in from the fanlight at the front door. When you knocked on Mr O'Shea's door and he let you in, you would blink for a second. The whole front of the room was one large window through which poured sun or rain, or whatever weather Dublin was enduring.

Julia ran to the window to look down on the swans, the people hurrying along the streets on either side of the river. Usually, she came with Grandpan when he was getting a new jacket, which didn't happen very often, but this day the clothes were to be made for her. As he had told her aunt, her Grandpan was sending her back to England all equipped in good Irish tweed. Julia stayed at the window as the elderly men conversed with each other. Mr O'Shea was very small and always wore a tape measure around his neck and pins sticking out of his waistcoat.

Her grandfather called her over, and Mr O'Shea brought her to the back of the shop, pulled out rolls of cloth, and asked her which she would like. Julia could not summon up much enthusiasm. She knew these were for her new life in England. Still, she liked Mr O'Shea, so she looked carefully at the rolls of tweed and finally put her hand on a roll that was the colour of turf with black lines throughout. Mr O'Shea looked surprised.

'Would you not prefer a blue coat?' he moved along the shelf. 'There's a lovely heather tweed here?'

Julia shook her head. 'No, thank you, Mr O'Shea, I like this one. It reminds me of donkeys.'

'Well, it's a good choice, so,' he said, lifting her onto the table and measuring her from neck to knee and across her meagre chest. He scribbled in a worn notebook as he did so. 'Would you like a different material for the skirt?' Julia said she would like the skirt in brown, so he measured her for that. Then Mr O'Shea sat her by the window and gave her some biscuits. She tried not to think about being sent away. She concentrated on looking at the bracky river flowing ever onwards before her. Snatches of the talk came to her. She knew it must be about politics, for the words Connolly, Pearse, and Collins were to be heard as the two gentlemen relived old battles.

Mr O'Shea told her grandfather that the clothes should be ready in four days. He would start work on them immediately. A rush job. That's the day before I have to go, thought Julia. If he took longer, perhaps she would have to wait till the clothes were finished. She pulled at her grandfather's sleeve.

'Perhaps you shouldn't ask Mr O'Shea to hurry, Grandpan. He has a lot of work.' She pointed to the stiff horsehair models draped with material for men's suits and ladies' coats and capes.

Mr O'Shea heard her. 'Ah, now, child, you are not to worry. I would do anything for your grandfather, and I know he wants you to have good Irish clothes to go away in.'

'That is kind, thank you, Grandpan.' Defeat must be handled with good grace.

Mr O'Shea shook hands with her and then with her grandfather, and the two of them went back downstairs, Julia holding tight to her grandfather's hand. It had started to rain, so her grandfather hurried her away from the quays up Parliament street.

They climbed some imposing steps into a hotel. A trio of ladies in grey were playing music in a corner. One large lady had an enormous instrument, like an overgrown fiddle, in front of her. A wispy woman next to her had a middle-sized one. The dark-haired young girl at the end of the trio had what looked like an ordinary fiddle to Julia. They did not look up from their music, and Julia recognised the tunes they were playing on the radio. This one was 'Smoke Gets in Your Eyes'. It was a favourite of Dr O'Toole. He had told her that he had learnt to dance with it. Mrs O'Toole had added that he was a gorgeous dancer.

Julia supposed they were waiting for the rain to stop, but her grandfather took off his hat and went up to the desk and said to the lady sitting there that he wished to reserve a table for two for lunch if that was possible.

'Indeed it is, sir,' she said. 'Would you like to go in now?'

'Thank you,' said her grandfather. Julia looked at him. 'Does Mrs Walsh know we are not coming home for lunch?'

'She does indeed, Julia. I told her we would not be home till later.'

Julia said nothing but wondered what lay in store for the afternoon.

Julia had only been at a hotel dining room once before, when her father had taken the children on Peggy's sixth birthday. This restaurant was less glamorous, but Julia supposed it was just in the evening that people dressed up to go out. When her father had taken them, she had had to wear a gingham dress with a big bow at the back, and her hair had been tied in plaits around the head. Peggy had a new dress. It was dark blue with different coloured patterns on it. Diamonds, spades, hearts and clubs, like playing cards, Peggy had told her, and Julia, who was not on the whole fond of frocks, had been jealous of this one.

The hotel dining room had ladies in hats whispering together over lunch and serious-looking gentlemen, some eating alone, reading *The Irish Times* or the *Irish Press*. Julia was the only young person there, and the elderly waitress wore a white apron and frilly cap and insisted on giving Julia second helpings of roast chicken and jelly. The room smelt of smoke, and the panels around the wall had faded to a foggy creamy colour. All around the room were pictures of horses, and Julia's grandfather told her they were famous winners and named some of them for her. Over their table by the wall hung a picture of a horse with a plaited mane, his rider low on his back jumping a hedge.

Grandpan told her that the horse was called Golden Miller, had been bred in Ireland and won more races than any horse in history. Julia thought about Peggy and her pony riding. 'Are there girl riders in races?' she asked, but her grandfather said he didn't think so.

When they left the restaurant, they walked up to Dame Street and toward Trinity College. Julia thought they must be going down to Mr O'Sullivan's shop. He was a great friend of Grandpan's, and when they were together, she noticed that her grandfather's voice became so sing-song that it was hard to understand. That was because they were both from Kerry. Although Julia knew from holidays that Grandpan had been born across the border in Cork; she had been there with him and her father often and loved it. Her uncle and aunt had no children and spoiled her, and she was let run loose all day without having to bother about clean clothes or brushing her hair; if her mother were in Dublin on the return, she would complain bitterly about the state of Julia. Her mother, Julia knew, did not like farm life. Julia had heard auntie Nora tell her husband that Julia's mother had notions, and although she knew better than to ask what this meant, Julia knew it was not praise.

When they crossed the street from Trinity, her grandfather turned up towards Grafton Street. Julia was disappointed. She liked going to O'Sullivan's to look at oilskins and striped sheets. Grandpan had told her that Mr O'Sullivan had kept the price of things cheap so that everyone could afford to buy his sheets and lampshades. The shop was an Aladdin's Cave stretching back from the piles of silky eiderdowns and packets of linen tea cloths in the window to the recesses of the shop, where woollen blankets and floral ladies' fleece nighties and striped men's pyjamas were heaped on wooden tables.

'Where are we going, Grandpan?' asked Julia. She was sucking a mint that he had produced from his pocket.

'We are going to buy shoes for you, Julia,' Grandpan replied.

Julia looked down at her black Mary Janes. She only wore them going out. At home she had plimsolls. 'New shoes,' she said?

They had turned up into Dawson Street. Grandpan stopped before a shop window with white communion shoes, pink ballet slippers, red tap shoes, lace-up shoes, and ladies' shoes, some with very high heels, in the window. There were no plimsolls to be seen.

'I'm not going to have to do ballet in England, am I?' she said. Rosa had shown her ballet dancers in comics and sighed and said she would like to be a ballerina, but she didn't think she was tall enough. Julia had not been very interested.

'No,' said Grandpan, 'we are getting you good outdoor shoes.'

They went into the shop. A bell jangled overhead as they went through the door, and a young woman in a neat blue suit and shoes of some furry material came forward to greet them.

'May I help you, sir?'

Grandpan explained that he was looking for shoes for his granddaughter.

'Party shoes?' the girl asked, but Grandpan told her she needed good strong shoes of leather that would not let in the rain.

The young woman sat Julia down and asked her to slip off her shoes, which Julia did, revealing a rather dirty white sock. The assistant put Julia's foot up on a board thing and, using a slide on it, measured Julia's foot. Then she disappeared to the back of the shop and returned teetering under boxes she held under her chin.

'Would the young lady have a preference?' she said and pulled out black lace-up and brown brogues and shoes the colour of chestnuts with a buckle at the front. Julia liked these the best. She tried them on, and they fitted perfectly, but Grandpan said she needed something stonger, so she tried on the brown pair and the black. Then Julia chose the brown to match her coat. Not all the clothes in the world would cheer her up, but she knew when she was beaten and that only being older would give her the chance to live as she wished and to be with her grandfather.

Grandpan told Julia to keep the new brown shoes on and asked the lady to put her old shoes in the box. 'Am I not to keep them for the journey?'

'No, pet, I'll explain.' He told the lady that he would take the shoes with the buckles as well. 'You will probably be going to parties with your sister,' he said.

'I don't want to go to parties,' said Julia, but she said it under her breath.

Out in the street, Grandpan told her to walk slowly and scuff the bottoms of her shoes along the pavement.

'Whatever for? Everyone will be looking at me?'

'No they won't. They are all too busy hurrying to wherever they are going. Give them a good scuff.'

Julia obediently skated up the street nearly as far as Stephen's Green and then back down to where her grandfather was waiting for her outside St Anne's church. She sat down on the steps. Her grandfather had wiped them with a hanky first. He examined the shoes closely and professed himself satisfied. He undid the other bag, and Julia put on the buckle shoes and skated and scraped her way up Dawson Street again, though she felt it was a pity to spoil such new things. Back at the church, she put her Mary Janes on and carried one of the bags as they walked towards the bus stop for Rathmines.

'Thank you for the shoes,' said Julia, 'but why did you want me to get them dirty?'

Grandpan explained. 'It is for the customs, Julia. Sometimes they don't like you to have new things, so it's better if they look used.'

Julia nodded. She understood all about the customs. Her mother, on her last visit, had collected jewellery from a shop in Clarendon Lane that her husband had bought for their wedding anniversary. Julia remembered the heavy necklace with the matching earrings and bracelet. Her mother had worn them at supper, and Julia thought them too bright in the dining room when they had their tea. When her mother was packing, Julia had seen her stuffing the jewellery into her underclothes. Peggy, who was helping, had fastened the earrings to her liberty bodice. Afterwards, Julia had asked her why they were doing that. Peggy had said it was because the customs men would have taken the jewellery if they had seen it. Julia had been horrified.

'Perhaps they will make Mummy take her dress off. And the customs men would find her jewels. I don't think she will be very good at hiding things.'

'Mummy looks very respectable,' said Peggy loftily. 'They wouldn't dream of searching her underclothes, and they won't go near me. I'm a child.'

'Supposing they fell out of your liberty bodice?' Julia had asked.

'Don't be silly,' said Peggy, lifting her Fair Isle sweater. 'I'm practising,' and she had showed Julia the black velvet pouch pinned on the inside of her vest.

Turning into the green, Julia asked her grandfather, 'What would the customs do if they guessed my shoes were new? Would they say I had to stay in Dublin?'

'Not at all, Julia. You must not worry. They might take them from you, though, and I promised Aunt Elizabeth that I would send you off in a tidy fashion. Perhaps don't tell her you got two pairs of shoes. She would think it extravagant of me,' replied her grandfather.

'Is Aunt Elizabeth coming to stay?' asked Julia, not relishing the prospect.

Her grandfather said evenly, 'I had a letter from her. She thinks I might need help getting you ready for the journey, and she will probably be here at the weekend.'

Julia thought that Aunt Elizabeth could ruin her last free days with Grandpan and Mrs Walsh. 'Could you not tell her that we are too busy? I mean, the General and Mrs General are coming to tea. I have to see Sandra and Rosa too, because she will be back from the seaside tomorrow. Dr O'Toole told me. I want to do everything we usually do.'

'We can still do them,' said Grandpan. 'Sure what's to stop us?'

Julia knew that Mrs Shannon would organise them to death and there would be no rides allowed on the milk dray or visits up the lanes.

'She can only stay a night,' said her grandfather. 'I told her there was no need to come.'

'She doesn't like you to be put upon,' Julia repeated a phrase often on Aunt Elizabeth's tongue and which always referred to Julia's presence in the house.

The number 15 bus snorted round the corner. The noise it made always reminded Julia of elephants in the zoo. She loved it when it was winter and evening. The bus lights would come looming out of the dark, and Grandpan would sit upstairs with her. They would look down on the city, the grey buildings, the humpy bridge over the canal, and the smell of fog and bodies and cigarettes, making the inside of the bus feel very comforting. Mrs Walsh would never sit upstairs. Rough boys were there. Julia and her grandfather never had any trouble with them. The bus lurched up into Harcourt Street. Julia peered out the window to see if the large tabby cat was in the window of the house of the famous actress who lived there. Julia longed to see the actress. She had seen pictures of her in the paper, but she was always in a shawl, so Julia did not know if she would recognise her in real life. The cat was there washing its face, and as the bus rumbled past on the other side of the road, Julia saw a tall woman in a beautiful green suit with red hair piled on top of her head come out of the house. The lady stood on the top step while she peered into her handbag. Julia shook her grandfather's arm.

'Is that the actress?' she asked, but the bus had already turned the corner.

Éilís Ní Dhuibhne

GLEANN BHAIRR

Beyond the bridge that spans the river Lennon
Three or four roads can take me to Portsalon
But I always drive the long way through Glenvar
The place my sinsear lived for centuries.
A mile from Kerrykeel the bungalows and trees
Give way to wilderness
A heath with not a soul or sheep in sight.
It's no surprise to see the sign then, on the bleak boreen:
'An Ghaeltacht'
This is the kind of place you often find it
Perched on a slope of bracken, furze, and heather
Heralding some storm-swept stony glen
cut off from English, and all that it implies.
And, always, beautiful.

DÚN CHAOIN

My house is a yacht on a sea
Of grass and gorse
Buttercups and dandelions.
It doesn't move
Across the waves
But the wild west wind
Rips its sails and tears its hair out.
My house is a boat
On a sea of heather and gorse.
I have to paint it every year
With yacht oil and grease
Just to keep it afloat.
My house is a ship
Moored to a sea
Of thistles and grass.
It shudders and shakes
But stays in its place.
The ocean comes to me.

SWEET SORROW

How quiet the house is!
It abhors a vacuum.
The second the last guest left
The dam burst
And deep silence flooded
Every room and cranny.
I was out on the driveway
Hugging and kissing
Then waving and waving
Until the car turned the corner.
When I stepped back in
The house felt like a museum.
It was like a house of the dead
Where a family had lived
A hundred years ago.
Their toys on display.
Their books never read.
And my heart was compressed
By a ring of iron.
The ring of sorrow.
Work should help.
I cleared the table
Where they had the last lunch.
Then took the red cloth out to the garden
To shake out the crumbs.
The garden was living.
Birds hopped on the gravel
Chipmunks and squirrels.
For days they have been hiding.
Days when the garden was loud
With the laughter of children.
Their running and singing.
The garden abhors a vacuum.
It's filled with sweet sounds.

Helena Nolan

A KISS ON THE BRIDGE

* *Photo of a couple kissing on the Imjingak observation post*
overlooking the demilitarised zone between North and South Korea.
The park was built to console those from both sides who are unable to
return because of the division of Korea and is home to the Bridge of
Freedom.

The bridge is a place between territories
A moment when we are unsure
Whether to cross, whether to touch

The bridge divides our countries
One landmass becomes two
Because of it, joined but separate

You lean towards me and
All the weight of centuries is on your back
Forcing apart your shoulder blades

You cannot see my face, instinct will tell you
How to bend low and find my lips
Strange yet familiar

Perhaps we are related, some long distance
Cousins, divorced by space and time, a history
Here reunited

The bridge is a spine, rippling beneath my feet
Like the river tide until
Your shadow swallows mine.

* *From a photograph in the* Sunday Independent, *7 April 2013*

In the centre of the building, caged in glass, is a glinting
lozenge
A gift, the shape of a luggage tag, lobed handle still ready
To be hung from clothing or slung round the neck of an
explorer
Trader, traveller, sponsored adventurer, in undiscovered
lands.
Stamped in its gold are symbols, seeking safe passage and
our hope
Must be that a thing so strange and beautiful did convey both
The message and the man, and was not pilfered for its
weight or
Worse, repurposed, metal seized by force, turned to a
weapon.

It glows now, a totem of good faith, the words – *By the
strength of eternal Heaven* – carved in its side, a gilded
passport set in a
Transparent cage, chained like the goldfinch in the
painting to its
Constant perch, relic of Khan and Xanadu, vanished, long-
decayed.
On darker days our senses seek it, as we pass, sometimes
even
Imagining a sign that says, 'In case of emergency, break
glass.'

*Kubla Khan issued a golden tablet (paiza in Chinese, gerege in Mongolian) a
foot long and three inches wide and inscribed with the words 'By the strength
of the eternal Heaven, holy be the Khan's name. Let him that pays him not
reverence be killed.' The golden tablet was effectively the first diplomatic
passport, authorising travellers to receive such horses, lodging, food and
guides as they required. A golden paiza was gifted by Mongolia to the IAEA
and is on display in the main concourse, where it tends to go largely
unnoticed.*

Clairr O'Connor

VOICES FROM AN INVASION (1956)

1 *The Key*
Always I hear your voice.

'Do not succumb.
Those complicit compromises
were betrayals, not prescience
no matter what they say now.
Move towards a composed
intelligence. Veer to happiness,
solace, not least from dusk
to dark. Choose memories
which energise. Press on.
If you step on your dipped
hem, get up. Fast. Move.'

There is compression
of days without tight focus.
The world disarticulated.
Times when I can't
bear to face myself
in a mirror though
no one else is here.
What I want
most is a
reckoning.
Yet, all there is ...
is time and use.
Destruction.

On those days I avoid
the caged lift. My muscles
burn by the time I reach

the door. I drop the string bag
and insert the big black key.

2 *March*

Unnerved, outraged. A wheeze in my chest.
The rusty results of my constant cough
poppy the snow. No bullet in my back
as yet. Not long ago there was still
hope. Days or weeks since I saw a
treeline? To see branches moving—
something to break up this white freeze
that shivers through the body. The guard
kicked his irritation out; a few ribs broken.
No road, no verges. Nothing widens or narrows.
I recall the condensation on the windows
as Klotild and I sipped hot chocolate
from red mugs in winter.

Movement burns in pain.
Broken shoes seep, snow-wet.
My head is heavy as rock,
rimed in frost. Each unwilled
step a torture. We are stumbling
towards an iron world.

3 *Wander*

When Grandmother first began to wander,
scraps of purpose led her to the market:
still securing the cheapest cuts, sweetest
carrots, freshest eggs whose gold
dribbled our breakfast plates.

She didn't care for city streets
hurrying to Keleti to board the train
back to her interrupted country life.
A slower reluctance each time she
returned to Bajza. At first I didn't notice.

Karo's absence filled my days,
felled my nights. I ate on the hoof
or picked at offerings from her
pot when I remembered.
She rambled in a mist all hours
barely sitting for supper.

She searched for fragments,
talked of father's boyhood
in the forest by the river.
Sometimes she forgot his death.
Expected him for dinner

I visited everyone Karo knew.
Some would not speak.
Those who spoke had nothing
to say. There was no rest.
Always something withheld.

Came the day when Grandmother
could neither go nor stay.
That foggy night they came to meet
me in the courtyard as I returned.
The police had been. They found
her under the Debrecen train.

Mary O'Donnell

WHITE GIRL INFERNOS

In Elias Canetti's novel *Auto-da-Fé* (1935), the protagonist, sinologist Peter Kien, goes insane for his obsessive love of books, which ultimately are the cause of his death in a massive conflagration of pages and print. This was Canetti's first and only novel, for which he won the Nobel Prize in 1981 and, interestingly, it was part inspired by the fire in Vienna's Palace of Justice in 1927. What affected him so greatly was the fact that, notwithstanding the deaths of countless people in the flames, a clerk was running around wailing about 'the wonderful files, the wonderful files!' And that inspired the creation of Peter Kien, one of the most unstable, focused, obsessive characters in early twentieth-century literature.

I have often thought about this novel, and the manner in which we sometimes fence ourselves off – albeit in more harmless ways – from what we find to be threatening, or intolerable, or indefensible. That habit began in childhood for me, when I was happily embedded in rural Monaghan, an only child receiving the best of my parents' attentions in my early years just outside the town, in Tullyherim. It lay a half mile from the creamery, where my father was general manager. My first five years were spent there, in Fern Villa, a three bedroomed, two-storey rented house that belonged to the Bishop of Clogher. It had a garden at the front with unwieldy evergreens on an uneven lawn. The back of the house led to the River Blackwater, the singing flow of which I can still hear as it made its way northwards towards the Bann and on to Lough Neagh.

While in Tullyherim I was cocooned in my parents' general approval of me. In some respects, my mother put my father on a pedestal, something women tended to do all his life. Charming and engaging, he had the gift of making people always feel included in whatever was going on. Special puddings were created for him, and I was aware of his likes and dislikes, not because he made any particular fuss about this but because my mother, who came from a family in which things revolved around men, was used to catering to their whims and needs. I retain a vivid memory of an iced rich fruit birthday cake for him, white with blue-scrolled writing and curlicues, created with all the energy and aesthetic perfectionism of the nineteen-fifties housewife. That cake sprang to mind when I watched *The Hours* based on Michael Cunningham's novel, and observed the struggles of an American housewife as she tries to make the perfect birthday cake for her husband and ends up putting the whole thing in the kitchen trash.

There was urgency to getting things right for middle-class women in the fifties and my mother was no exception. Whether in fashion or household matters, progress was in the air, like a pollen, and it was expected that the bleak and grey years of the Emergency and immediate post-war were no more. For un-bohemian women outside the exempting protection of artistic practice (because it was accepted that bohemians were free thinkers and didn't have to conform), women like my mother in other words, what else could they want, other than a good home, and the chance to keep it, to gild the cage and to feed the occupants well?

Yet there were some fantastic misfits around our town, women who tried to conform but couldn't, women who just weren't bothered, or women like my mother, anti-authoritarian by nature, who lived within the span of the frowning world of Catholic Ireland, yet were silently at odds with its illogical demands. There were all kinds of women on the loose within the tight little world of our town: a woman who wrote and wrote while her children lived in a state of benign neglect; a woman with a drink problem who, it was said, didn't bother with underwear, top or bottom, which created some clucking among the town matrons. Only the aristocracy, or semi-aristocracy were allowed to go knicker-less, it seemed. A grand aunt who was a seamstress talked about one of the county grandees from Castle Leslie who once arrived for a fitting, with, as she said 'a high English accent and no knickers'.

The moment my father went off to work in the black Morris Minor – either heading straight to the office or driving out into the country to visit various branch creameries which came under the central creamery's remit – I was left with my mother, whose routines were very different, and whose moods too were very different. She was a colourful spectrum of sometimes unrealised dreams, of romanticism, mixed, in her case, with a strong Ulster pragmatism. Only in adult life did she begin to pursue the education that, for a number of reasons, did not come her way when she was younger. For one thing, she was lazy; for another, she got little encouragement. But she read extensively. She liked to cook and to sing. She enjoyed fashion. Once, I awoke when my parents came home after a night out at a dinner-dance. She wore a long pale-pink gown, like watered silk. It shimmered in the light, the neckline falling low in soft folds. A pair of silvery high-heeled evening shoes glittered on her feet, the kind most little girls adore. She looked radiant and glamorous, and I felt so happy with my mother and her beauty.

On another occasion, I observed her having her morning bath, slushing the water in waves over her legs as she opened and closed them, playing in the water. That was also the day I saw red liquid falling from her as she sat on the lavatory, and asked what it was. Whatever she mumbled I no longer remember, only the sight of this arresting red. But I wasn't concerned or anxious. It wasn't a cut or an injury, and she seemed perfectly well.

The question of physical differences arise early in life. My parents were free and easy in their domestic habits and bathrooms were not places in which locks were turned or privacy sacrosanct. Nakedness was natural in the household at certain times. In the same way, it was in the bathroom that I discovered my father's penis. He too was sitting on the lavatory but when I pointed and asked him what that thing was, he shooed me out of the bathroom. I remember it as clearly as if it was one of those Japanese fertility fetishes found around certain shrines, a thing in itself, quite separate from his general body.

Next door, Maurice Graham was sixteen and still at school in the Collegiate. He would race on the path to his home in a black school uniform with red trim, school tie undone. School was something I looked forward to, without knowing that it would be the seedbed of so many great fears for a number of years. His brother Roy brought me a basket of chocolate Easter eggs, nestling in straw, with small yellow chicks beside them, for my fourth birthday. Slightly spoiled and already self-possessed, I promptly rejected these with a sour 'Don't want them' and was instantly scolded by my mother then made to apologise. That was obviously one of my off-days, because an uncle had also bought me a pair of black patent-leather shoes. I disliked them on sight and was possessed by an urgent feeling that they had to be got rid of, whatever the means. The feeling is as strong now as it was then, that if necessary, I have the agency to eradicate the seriously dislikeable. When the adults were out of the way, I crouched down before the open fire in the sitting room and threw the shoes onto the burning coals. I watched a moment for them to take, then sat on my hunkers as the flames began to lick at the shining patent leather. It was too late by the time anyone discovered what was happening, and by then the fire was a merry melt roaring up the chimney.

I don't recall the fall-out from that particular event, but it does make me wonder about the character of a child, and how definite and defined it is from birth and even from before birth. I'm convinced that children's decisions are made in the light of particular tastes, wants and feelings, some of these more oppositional than adults are capable of understanding. We are all contrarian beings at times and I must have been pretty crabbed about something that day to reject the Easter eggs and at the same time to throw a pair of shining new shoes on the blazing coals.

To this day, I enjoy burning things that I want rid of. It's the ultimate solution with a long and interesting history. When one considers the book burnings, the genocides, the razings mandated by the dictators and disapprovers of history, one realises that the instinct to obliterate is an instinct forged deeply in the human psyche, often perverted into a cunning and undermining destructive force. Unfortunately, there seem to be no 'good' burnings aimed at something positive – at least none that I can recall

– and all I can think of is the burning of the great library of Alexandria, books and art burned by Hitler, the burning of the palace of Justice in Vienna, and the behaviour of various Chinese emperors. Later, I was to burn love letters and photographs, and anything too painful to be tolerated any longer. I always imagine I will keep things as 'keepsakes', but in the end I don't, not if things have turned out very badly.

My most significant burning was to culminate in a thick wad of letters from a prisoner in a jail in Atlanta, Georgia, with whom I'd corresponded for some months after answering a pen-friend ad in the evening paper. I was nineteen. His name was Melvyn J. Hall. After several letters had been exchanged, he eventually revealed his true state of being, as a prisoner, and how he spent his days in the State penitentiary. I continued to write, mostly from a sense of excitement at being in touch with a real, black prisoner. I was a typical little white girl, world-starved, and my imagination rocketed at the prospects of having my very own Sidney Poitier to write to. The man was thirty-three and by his own account was serving seven years for bank robbery. He was due out in some months. His letters entranced and flattered me. I didn't realise how heavily time weighs on a prisoner, how many hours are available for the writing of letters and imagining a new future. His were extensive and beautiful, and I was flattered by his use of a word like 'pulchritude' to describe my beauty as he saw it.

Paradoxically, by then I'd read *Black Skin, White Masks* by Frantz Fanon. I had actually half-absorbed the now classical analysis of the relationships between white men and black women, and between white women and black men, and expectations and stereotypes prevailing on both accounts. But even so, I hadn't the sense to analyse Fanon's text in the way it deserved, and it seemed remote and untranslatable in terms of from my own, intimacy-starved life. I was an inexperienced virgin, white to the core, trying to push away from what was white, virginal, inexperienced, familiar, parochial, narrow and boring. I needed excitement, newness and danger, without knowing exactly what that meant. I knew little about men's bodies or minds, having no brother. With every letter, my imagination flew to the clouds. When Melvyn got out of prison, I thought, we would meet, and who knew what could happen then?

Finally, he sent a photograph. Reality kicked in (he hadn't rushed at an exchange of photographs, but early on I'd enclosed a flattering image of myself). I felt ashamed at my reaction. I felt ashamed at the knowledge that I had been raising the hopes of this incarcerated man who was also looking for something new and perhaps healing for himself. He stood, with fine, broad nostrils and thick lips, his skin shiny, in a prison uniform. He was what all of us can be if you strip away the adornments and artificial little ruses with which we decorate ourselves every single day in the outside world. No, he was more than that and I did not find him in any way physically attractive. Despite this reaction and what followed, I recognised how shallow I was. Behind him in the photo loomed the backdrop of a grey block concrete wall. His world, I realised, was utterly frightening, all too adult, and light years beyond my capacities.

I knew that not in a million years would I ever be able to meet him, that the prospect of him turning up in Dublin would horrify me. In a way, he was above me, too good for me, too rich with an armoury of experience that was beyond me. What would we possibly have to say to one another? How could I hold his hand, or even more, kiss him? At the same time, I knew I was despicable, having raised this man's hopes. I would have to be sexually attracted to anyone I was going to meet in a romantic context, and I found Melvyn unattractive.

I wrote the letter, my final one, inventing feeble excuses about why I could no longer correspond. I was going to university, I waffled. I was very busy. My father was ill. I would be very busy for the foreseeable future once I went to university. This relationship had to be eradicated from my reality and day-to-day life, and completely and utterly from my consciousness. By now, I was on the run and found the mere idea of Melvyn unbearable. There could be no further trace of it, anywhere. I posted the letter in Donnybrook, not far from the house I was renting with a few other girls.

His reply was lengthy and ferocious, hurt and justifiably wrathful. He said that, on reflection, when he regarded my photograph all he could see was hatefulness in my visage, and no sign of pulchritude, the Latinised word he used. He said much more, but I don't remember it all, as he struck back at me with phrase after phrase, outlining the failure and misery of my being. I deserved to burn in hell, he added. The gist of it was that he saw through my silly posturing, but that he would be coming to Ireland anyway, to meet a more mature woman with whom he was corresponding.

Some of what Melvyn wrote in this final outpouring was true. Some of it was not. Of course, I was not the devil incarnate as he implied. I was not many of the negatives he heaped on me in his rage. But neither was I without blame. In the end, I turned to fire again and burned those letters. I gathered up the months of his writings, five or six months of fine blue-papered writing in his elegant, forward-slanting hand, with its rich and poetic vocabulary, often praising and flattering me beyond recognition, so much more than I deserved, and carried them home with me one weekend. I slipped out the back door of my parents' house (they were now in a different house, further out the country) and set out for the orchard. I laid the letters in the long summer grasses and tangled nettles some distance away from the trees with their ripening Bramleys. Then I lit a match and burned the lot.

It took a number of matches before the mass of thin blue paper blazed blue, red, orange, yellow, green and finally to a crescendo of dancing red. Perfection. The only solution, to obliterate all physical evidence of what had occurred, to annihilate, do whatever necessary to remove from the material world all that challenged me and that I was too overwhelmed to face. And although I have burned things at intervals throughout my life, I know, as anyone in tyrant-mode knows, that nothing is ever eradicated for good. Everything lives on. After all, because the books at Alexandria were so ferociously and deliberately burned, or because certain Chinese emperors also ordered book and manuscript burnings, and because Hitler attempted to entirely remove a race of people by burning them, we are all the more capable of remembering. What is incinerated enters a groove in the psyche, like the grooves in an old vinyl record, where the whole inferno can be played and replayed again and again. Until full recognition occurs? Perhaps.

It's all a long way from the fictional burning of Canetti's crazed Peter Kien's library, and longer indeed from my own private childhood burning of the shoes, but it tells me something today about my own insistence, every so often, in doing precisely what I believe to be the necessary thing in order to survive. It's a pattern I was to repeat throughout my life, and the knowledge of that insistence on following my own lodestone – even if it's not always admirable – has sometimes been the saving of me.

Beth O'Halloran

THE REUNION

In standstill traffic, Helen's mother, Dot, leans across her to check her lipstick in the little mirror above the glove compartment. 'Ever notice how the driver's seat doesn't have one?' she says to Helen, who never had. 'That's because it's supposed to be husbands driving wives who have free hands to powder whatever they please.'

These are new things Helen's mother says now that Helen is an adult and her mother can open the window to what early widowhood had meant.

They have pulled into the parking lot of a *monstrosity of a mall* so that Dot can buy Helen something to wear that might be a bit *less derelict* – for dinner at Rick's country club because he's sure to suggest it. June sun blares in ripples from the hoods of parked cars.

It has been twenty-one years since the man in the driving seat died. And in that time Helen's mother has not so much as skimmed another man's hand, but some months back, an expert talking head was needed for a TV interview on the historical conservation impacts of *the great big purple eyesore of a bank they slapped right where there used to be a perfect view of the river.* Helen watched the clip several times, curious at her mother's capacity of swallowing her honesty.

The news clip went to the Tri-state area. Which is how her ex-beau, as she called him, had known where to find her. 'Golly, I guess more than forty years, Rick.' There were many more phone calls and letters. She used the tissue-y paper embossed with her initials in blue.

Dot insisted that it would be improper to meet Rick without a chaperone, so when the opportunity arose, with Helen finishing college for the summer, it was decided that they would drive from Washington DC to Maine via Rick's place in Connecticut – and they would spend the night.

Not even a splinter of shade in this godforsaken lot. Helen glances at the spindly trees. They park in the shadow of a van with an image of peaches painted on it. Each peach has a droplet of water gliding down its sumptuous curves. Helen's hair is stuck to her face like a cobweb. The walk to the mall entrance seems to take a very long time. There is a sound of a cricket coming from a shrivelled shrub. The cool, cold even, mall air makes them lift their heads as if they have come from something very dense and dark.

Helen pulls back the changing-room curtain to a too bright light. This is dress number four. Helen now feels like a spindly tree. Dot moves her jaw left and right. 'Well it'll have to do. I just don't understand why you can't try something that doesn't say 'why bother?' Something with even a shred of hopefulness in it.'

Helen says, 'When you get to wondering why I'm not skidding home for Thanksgiving, please remember this entire event.'

'Good grief. Since when is it a cardinal offence to want a little cheer in a wardrobe? Don't you ever get tired of wearing black?'

'Everything goes together when it's black.'

'Mnnn ... like wet rags and misery.' They both snort at that.

They are back on the highway, windows open, air thrumming, a square of blistering heat on Helen's arm. Their Subaru sways each time an eighteen-wheeler overtakes them. She has her seatbelt fastened. Dot has not. Dot is wishing they could've taken the back roads *that let you see a scrap of life*. She announces each link – 'There it is – the Baltimore-Washington Parkway. Give me notice this time or we're liable to miss the Hutchinson River Parkway exit. Jeesh, I remember when that wasn't more than a rickety bridge over a creek. What a mouthful.' Helen turns on the radio. A panpipe version of Simon & Garfunkel's hammer and nail/sparrow and snail. Helen is wishing many things.

'I'm just surprised you never told me you'd been engaged to him before Dad, that's all.'

'Well, I didn't see what good it would do,' says Dot as she swats at something. 'At long last, there's the Oak Street Connector for New Haven. Although why they still call it Oak Street is a mystery of course.'

'It just would've been nice to know that I'm about to meet a man who might well have been my father, had you not done that senior year in Ireland.' Helen has a fold-out map on her lap – completely folded out despite only needing one little manageable panel now that they are near. She wishes she could origami a tent out of the whole thing.

'So, how are your courses going anyway?' asks Dot.

'OK, I guess. Glad it's summer. I'm already dreading the thesis next year.'

'It seems strange to make art college kids write such a substantial text.'

Helen glances at her mother. 'Yeah, it can kind of take you out of the whole thing, by writing about it, y'know.'

'I'm not sure I know what you mean by 'the whole thing' but I'm sure you're perfectly capable, once you apply yourself.'

They have pulled onto the hard shoulder to study the map. The car is instantly a furnace.

'It just would've been nice to know, that's all.'

There is much rustling as Dot leans across, yet again, to pout and touch up her lipstick. 'Oh Helen, you brood too much. What's the point in saying things that don't need to be said.'

'Right,' says Helen.

Helen has never seen her mother apply lipstick more than once in the same day. As she sits back into her own seat, Dot glances at Helen. 'For the love of Pete, will you tidy that mop on your head – maybe a side parting. That middle-part ... just, no. You look like the village idiot.'

Helen slides her loose hair behind her ears, folds the map and says, 'I can't understand why you won't wear your seatbelt.'

'You know full well that thing cuts me in two.'

Each house looks like a diplomat lives in it. There are white columns, flags stirring limply in the heat. After a very long, slowed-down drive that makes the cars speed past them in an exaggerated curve, a mailbox with the right number on it peeks out from a cloud of hedge. Rick's drive looks like a country lane and is as overgrown. He is waiting out front, waving in big arcs. The air is blurred with small flying things. He is grinning. Dot is grinning back while rubbing her forefinger across her thumb in very small circles. Helen can hear her mother's swallow as she opens the car door and eyes the figure who is as groomed as a pilot. 'You look really nice.' Helen has the sense to stay in the car.

His long arms are in a crisp white shirt. 'Oh, Dot, aren't you a picture.'

Helen tugs their overnight bags out of the backseat and is trying to close the car door with her knee, when Rick appears at her elbow, takes both bags, and says, 'Allow me.'

'Thanks.' And for a moment Helen imagines Rick as her father. What a comforting voice he has. All news-castery. They walk towards his porch, its paint so bright it looks charged. She feels slightly winded.

'I hear you're quite the artist. Your mom sent me clippings. Oils or watercolours?'

'She did?' Her swallow has gone hard. 'Wow, this is a beautiful house.' Dot is standing in the hall, beaming, watching them cross the threshold. 'I can manage the bags now, Rick, thanks. Upstairs I assume?' He touches the back of Helen's head with such tenderness, she feels as though she is a small child.

Rick's hallway has one of those staircases you see in big-city libraries – the kind that has white bannisters and starts off as one flight but then fans off into two with a stained-glass window at the landing making the whole thing look like a bird with its chest puffed out.

Helen drifts to a window that's about the size of her bedroom back in the city. Outside, there is a garden where she can't tell where lawn ends and flowerbeds begin as things have outgrown their borders. The contrast to the house's fresh white façade confuses Helen. A kidney-shaped swimming pool is covered in clots of green algae. When she lifts her hands from the windowsill, she leaves their exact shape in the dust.

Rick hollers up, 'There are two powder rooms down the hall. Set yourself up wherever you like.'

She finds a pink room – curtains and frothy bedspreads like a birthday cake.

'How about we wet our whistles?' says Rick as he guides them towards a living room that looks over the garden. He makes cocktails in crystal glasses that bounce rainbows whenever he shifts.

There is a lamp on a floor where there should have been a side table and Helen guesses Rick's wife got it in the divorce. Dot's eyes scan a kitchen sink full of plates and takeaway boxes. When she sees the garden, she says, 'Such a lot of house, Rick, now that your girls are at college.'

Rick stirs the ice in his glass with his middle finger. Helen wonders if Dot finds the action stirring, which makes Helen want to think about anything else. He's at home in his skin, this tall, handsome man. His bookshelves are full of history and biographies. Dot reads nothing else – *Why waste time on made-up stories when history is so riveting?* He talks about how hard it has been to sell the house. Helen catches, 'local real estate market' ... 'total demographic shift at the campus' ... 'affirmative action BS.' Dot looks sharply at the carpet, for she does not use any form of *colourful* language. 'There was a sale that got side-railed at the last minute, but that's a long story.' He winks at this. Helen wonders if perhaps Rick knows how to make even a short story long, but Dot crosses her ankles and says, 'Yes, it's such a hardship when you are dependent on outside factors.'

Helen studies silver-framed photographs on the mantelpiece. His daughters are so lovely, Helen at first imagines they are the perfect black and whites that come in the frame – the surf and clapboard houses in the background. Even a beaming Labrador flopped at the girls' bare feet. Dot's catchphrase – whenever the subject of divorce is raised – *the mystery of squandered happiness.* Helen glances back at her mother, who had adored her father. The night of the accident, she had been holding off feeding their brood until he got back from night school. Dot was called to the morgue to identify him, but his injuries were so severe, they only let her see his hands.

After their second cocktail, Dot looks at her watch twice a minute. With the third drink, it's clear they are not going to any country club for dinner. Helen says, 'Why don't you two chat and I'll rustle up something for dinner.' In the kitchen, she opens cupboards full of boxes with nibbled corners. Contents of the fridge are a small carton of half-and-half, a shrinking lemon and something brown in Saran Wrap. Eventually, she finds cans of tuna and tomatoes. And some spaghetti. While stirring, Helen imagines Dot and the other country club dinners she never got to go to.

She can hear Rick looking for something. 'Oh no you don't,' says Dot. 'I won't remember a soul.' But she does remember. While the pasta is boiling, Helen goes back to the sitting room, but hesitates in the doorway. The two of them are sitting on a two-seater sofa, turning the pages of his album. 'Honey, come see this.' It is a photograph of Dot and Rick standing outside. His hand is at Dot's waist. Helen studies the image – sure enough there's an unfamiliar, hulking diamond ring on her mother's finger. It is remarkable how happy her mother looks, both in the photo and now. 'Heavens, were we ever that young, Rick?'

Helen doles out the pasta that looks like plane food. She puzzles over Rick's lack of preparation but thinks he's probably just distracted, excited even. They do not sit at Rick's twelve-seater dining table. Knee to knee, they put paper towels on their laps and take glances at the garden. The sun is dropping now, lighting the long grasses from behind. Helen did not change into her new dress for this dinner and worries that her jeans and navel-showing top will draw a concerned face from Dot, but Dot is leaning in to hear every word out of Rick.

Helen's attention dims so she's just catching pieces. 'Yes, lake house. Still there. New deck. Well, we'll just have to go back. You too, Helen.' Rick's voice is louder, thanks to the gimlets.

Dot is back on the subject of the house sale. 'Surely, you've had a lot of interest.'

'Yes, yes.' There is a ramble about a string of viewings which Helen misses until he says, 'Let me tell you, once I heard they were poofters, that was the end of that sale. Imagine.' Helen's chest feels vacuum-packed. Dot has long been a practising Catholic. Helen is not at all sure how her mother might feel about homosexuals buying a mansion in Connecticut.

'And it was a spot of luck, I do a few holes with one of their bosses and got to set him straight. Pardon the pun.'

The sun's dip reveals a mass of dead once-flying things caught in the window screen. In the distance, after many false starts, someone has started a high-pitched lawnmower. Helen wishes she knew how Dot now feels about this man – this unexpected miracle who might hold her hand into their last days. But just weeks ago, one of Helen's college friends had been beaten to a pulp for locking elbows with his boyfriend. They had just walked Helen to her bus stop, laughing and waving at her as her bus pulled away.

Her mouth like blotting paper. She gulps water as he says, 'Had to take it off the market for the summer. Hence the weed onslaught. Missed my window. You know how everyone packs up and heads upstate once the heat hits.'

Dot nods. She regularly complains about out-of-staters and their big-city habits being out of synch with Maine, where no one even locks their front door.

The lawnmower has neared the house. 'Did I misunderstand you, Rick?' asks Helen. Heads swivel. Her face hot. 'It's just that what I thought I heard you say was that you turned down an offer on this house, where you no longer want to live, because the would-be purchaser is a homosexual ... and then, you thought it would be best to let the man's employer know he is gay.' She cannot look at her mother as she adds, 'And, and if that *is* what you are saying, I just want to say ... to say ... that I'm appalled.' No one speaks for what feels like a full minute. Helen takes another sip of water and motions to lift her plate. 'I'm sorry. I'll just go clean this up.' As she rises to leave, she raises her eyes to Dot, but she is fingering her glass.

A dizzy feeling, Helen washes her plate and says goodnight but doesn't hear a response. She catches the word *sensitive* from Dot, which she has always used as a euphemism for cracker-jack crazy.

Sleep won't come. She can hear Rick's deep *haw, haw* laughs and her mother's too. The sound of a distant motorcycle threading through the darkness in the thick heat comforts Helen. She is thinking of her own father, who died while she was a baby. How many times had she longed for his legendary kindness. He had been an engineer – a builder of bridges and roads, someone who knew how connect things.

It is dawn now. The window framed in turquoise light. A rustling of a paper bag wakes Helen. Then the smell of coffee being held under her nose. Her mother hands her her glasses. 'Wow, what kind of time is it, Mum?'

'About five, I guess. I got you the coconut one.' She hands Helen a Dunkin' Donuts bag.

'You've already been out? And got us breakfast?'

'Well, I had trouble sleeping.'

'Me too, Mum. I'm sorry ...'

Dot raises her hand and makes a *shish* sound. 'Let's hit the road before he wakes up.'

'Without saying goodbye?'

'Yes, without saying goodbye.' Dot's voice is heavy, but clear.

Outside, the cool early morning air still smells of freshly cut grass. Carrying the bags back to the car, Helen studies her mother's face. Dot has paused and lifted her chin while a chickadee calls. She glances back at the house and quickly returns to her stride.

'Are you ok?'

'For heaven's sake, I'm fine. He was just looking for someone to take care of that mausoleum.' But the sink of loss has returned to Dot's eyes. 'That garden could've really been something, though ...'

'Yeah, it could've.'

The thrill of gingerly closing their car doors and creeping back down the lane, a haze ahead. Dot hands Helen the warm paper cup.

Anne Roper

AT THE SIDE OF A BED ...

I met the poets Eavan Boland and Sheila Wingfield within
a few months of each other. It was the mid-1980s and a
formative time for me. I was flushed with youthful ardour,
embroiled in a tumultuous love affair with poetry. Some
breadcrumbs of mine had been nibbled, then published. By
fluke a flat I shared in the late 1970s became the hub for a
nascent poetry enterprise. My housemate, the young poet
admin, was an early adopter of remote working. It meant
poetic men, celebrated or hopeful, sniffed around almost
daily, for news, connections or to chance their arm central-
casting for potential muses. We were Rubik's Cubes,
objects to be puzzled over and fixed into boxed notions of
'woman'. Frustratingly for the lads, we resisted. I was
naively confident we could become writers ourselves. Not
many of the guys agreed. In some way it explains why,
over the next years of braided paths, Sheila Wingfield and
Eavan Boland became such touchstones for me. At
different times and a generation apart, the two poets stuck

their heads above the fray. I would only learn of their fleeting yet resonating connection twenty years later.

Eavan Boland came first. In 1974, I'd settled in Ireland from America to study English in Trinity College, Dublin. Nannying, then waitressing late night in Grafton Street, paid my way. Eavan, an alumna of TCD, was the revered success amongst women with poetic aspirations. Her 1975 poem 'The Other Woman' would speak directly to my muse-full flat experiences, particularly as pursuing, albeit rebuffed poets, were often married men: 'How can I rival her/When like a harem wife she waits/To come into the pages of your novel/Obediently into your bed on nights/She is invited ...'

Seven years later it was *Night Feed* – although, having myself escaped a childhood rearing an army of younger siblings, the thought of domestic Dundrum life with bawling babies had a crippling, claustrophobic effect. Eavan's trajectory showed a woman could combine both roles of writer, mother. The success of her readings and teachings organised by Arlen House, the Irish women's press and its imprint Women's Education Bureau (WEB) became the proof.

In 1985, Arlen House and WEB announced that Eavan Boland would direct their first Annual Writers' Workshop for Women – the same year I stumbled across the poet Sheila Wingfield. It was also my last year working in the Dublin Well Woman Centre, then a rogue state of illegal condoms, feminist campaigning, IUDs and sperm banks. Not the stuff of poetry in an era of government bans and censorship.

One day during a weekly menopause clinic, I sat at the side of an examination bed waiting for the next client with my friend Moira Woods, the doctor on duty. As poetry was a joy we shared, I asked if Moira had a favourite. Immediately, she began reciting *Odysseus Dying* (1938): 'I

think Odysseus, as he dies, forgets which was Calypso,
which Penelope, only remembering the wind that sets off
Mimas, and how endlessly his eyes were stung with brine
...'

I'm fairly sure it was my first proper literary epiphany. I
loved it all: the precision, the circling beat, the immediacy,
the poignancy of loss, the confident ownership. But even
more I adored the hauling of classic mythology into an
ongoing and vibrating 'now'.

Moira told me the author was Sheila Wingfield (born
Beddington in 1906), better known as the Right
Honourable Viscountess, Lady Powerscourt. She was not
only a poet but chatelaine of Powerscourt House, an
eighteenth-century Anglo-Irish 'Big House' turned burnt-
pile in County Wicklow following a devastating fire in
1974. Sheila's mother's family were from Offaly. Sheila
would later claim they changed from Catholic to
Protestant under Cromwell's cudgel. In mid-twentieth-
century Ireland, the Powerscourt name still held a certain
cachet. Which was why, by the late 1950s, Moira
recognised Sheila while working as a young resident in
Baggot Street Hospital, a place Sheila booked into for
regular, prolonged periods of rest from uncertain illnesses.

During rounds, Moira would sit at the side of Sheila's
hospital bed as the two spoke of art and poetry. Moira was
half Sheila's age. Almost twenty years had passed since
Sheila's poems first appeared in *The Dublin Review* (1937).
Her work had been praised by W.B. Yeats, James Stephens
and John Betjeman. She would go on to publish eight
collections and three memoirs. *A Kite's Dinner* was selected
British Poetry Society Choice in 1954. Not surprisingly,
Moira found Sheila intelligent, curious and witty: 'She was
always impeccably dressed too,' despite her reclining,
Elizabeth Barrett Browning, posture. 'She would wear
different coloured peignoirs each day with coordinated

bed jackets in lemon or violet or bluebell – and always matching gloves.'

'Is she dead?' I asked, convinced the answer must be yes.

'I'm not sure, although you don't see many women poets in Ireland' – which was just the gnat of a challenge I needed to dig out my detective gear and begin searching.

By then I was learning that poetry could not yet fix Ireland's inequities nor its constitution – involvement in the 1983 abortion campaign being a case in point. Neither could poetry change discriminatory laws, cure gender disparity or make contraception fully accessible so that women could control their own bodies and lives. Hoping to address such issues in the era of Ann Lovett, Joanne Hayes and Eileen Flynn, I reviewed books on feminist studies for *The Irish Times*. Then, before I left the Well Woman, Attic Press published my book, *Woman to Woman* (1986), Ireland's (allegedly) first health and sexual care guide for women. Despite prohibitions I included names of chemists and clinics offering condoms, morning after pills or abortion information.

This was during the same period I applied for one of twelve places on an Arlen House/WEB women writers course run by Eavan Boland. At the time the opportunity of Eavan's guidance and the support of others on that journey was both an innovation and a considerable prize. From our first gathering in Blackrock, I remember Dolores Walshe, Éilís Ní Dhuibhne and Liz McManus. But mostly I was captured by Eavan and her confidence. She took us seriously. I was empowered by her passion and rigour, the same verve my friend Moira showed when she spoke of Sheila Wingfield.

But I also recognised something more familiar in Eavan: a tone and rhythm of speech that reminded me of America; a sense of kinship with her peripatetic childhood and how flux can disrupt a sense of home, place and identity. We shared an urge to question. Over the course of our weeks together, Eavan confirmed that, despite a dearth in the past, women's voices were required reading – and hearing – in a new Ireland.

What strikes me as curious now is that all that time we writers assembled in the sightline of the Sugarloaf and Powerscourt House, I never once mentioned, nor did it occur to me to ask Eavan about, Sheila Wingfield – a poet who had also struggled with many of the same themes of home, place, identity.

When the WEB course ended, many of us continued as a group which, I understand, endures to this day, although I left after eighteen months. Because of Eavan's encouragement, I had a short story published by Caroline Walsh in *The Irish Times*. More poetry and fiction was nurtured by Jessie Lendennie in *The Salmon*. I freelanced as a journalist. I also left the Well Woman to work on a Raidió Teilifís Éireann (RTÉ) TV book programme, *Bookside*, fronted by Doireann Ní Bhriain.

That's when I had a breakthrough in the hunt for Sheila Wingfield. Booksellers Bertram Rota in London put me in touch with David Pryce-Jones, former literary editor of *The Spectator* after landline calls rang out in an echoing Powerscourt House. It turned out Sheila was indeed alive and residing in the Swiss Ticino. Her address was the penthouse atop Hotel la Palma Au Lac on the shore of Lake Maggiore. Her 'final work', *Ladder to the Loft* (1987), was on the runway towards publication. I sent her a letter and almost immediately a telex arrived: 'Unable to travel being bed-ridden. Stop. Prefer personal interview. Stop. Could put you up here ...'

In April 1987, I flew to Zurich, then boarded a train to Locarno-Muralto, where Sheila's chauffeur collected me. Shortly after, like other women before me, I found myself sitting at the side of Sheila's bed in an apartment surrounded by books, a Rubens and a Ptolemaic carving of a man's head that reminded the poet of her father. Sheila Wingfield was then eighty, propped up in a double bed with views of the lake and mountains beyond – her appearance fragile, her spirit robust.

I'd brought copies of Sheila's out-of-print collections (she'd said she had none) along with Bewley's brown bread, Barry's tea and a week's worth of *The Irish Times*: 'I do miss it.'

She was also madly curious about Dublin. But more importantly, she wanted to know, 'Who is writing what?'

I told her about meeting other Irish women poets. I mentioned Eavan's course and that Eiléan Ní Chuilleanáin had lectured me in Trinity (spoiler alert: I may have called that course 'dead men's poetry'). Sheila regretted there hadn't been a sorority when she was young, although she appreciated Ottoline Morrell and Vita Sackville-West. Her loneliness perhaps leaned her into over-flattery: 'I seem only to have found a network recently, with David Pryce-Jones' support, and now you.'

A novel by Irving Wallace was propped on her bed tray. His Jewishness interested her. She resisted talking about her own. I'm not sure critical views of Sheila's work have fully appreciated the existential need she had to conceal that identity in her life and poetry. In 1930s and 1940s Europe, hiding for someone Jewish was a very real matter of life or death.

Ireland was not a safe haven either. Sheila's sense of outsider-ness, which Eavan also writes about, was not just as an 'Anglo' resident post-Civil War when Beddington and Powerscourt lands were compulsory purchased by the Free State. Ireland had its own brand of antisemitism. In 1906, the year Sheila was born, a violent pogrom of Jewish businesses in Limerick finally abated after most Jews left the city, cheered on by a Catholic priest. By 1932, when Sheila married in Jerusalem, the quasi-fascist Irish Blueshirts party (of which Yeats was an early fan) rose to 48,000 members. In a town where Jewish families were living eight kilometres from Powerscourt, a railway bridge was graffitied with 'Give us back Bray and we'll give you back Jerusalem' (*Something to Hide*, 2007). Meanwhile, writer and Wicklow neighbour, Francis Stuart, liaised with both the IRA and German military intelligence at the start of World War II. Stuart wasn't the only Irish citizen wondering whether the Reich might better aid Irish reunification than Britain.

Sheila hints at these anxieties in *Beat Drum, Beat Heart* ('In the dark of a room/Old fears were known'). New fears were made real when her father was killed at sea by German gunners in 1940 and her *husband*, Pat Wingfield, became a POW shortly afterwards. Is it any wonder the poet escaped to the safety of Bermuda before bombs fell on London, Belfast and Dublin? Any lessening of threat would only come later, suggested in poems like 'Waking', collected thirty years after the war's end:

When Lazarus
Was helped from his cold tomb
Into air cut by bird-calls
While a branch swayed
And the ground felt unsteady:
I must, like him, with all force possible
Try out my tongue again.

By 1987, on the edge of Lake Maggiore in neutral Switzerland and after introductory pleasantries were over, Sheila lifted a glass from her bed tray to make a toast before we started: 'I'm so nervous, I've had a brandy. I hope you don't mind?' And then, sitting on a stool at the side of her bed, I pressed record for my first interview with the Irish poet.

In our chats, Sheila said she loved beat more than rhyme and that people never quite 'got' *Beat Drum, Beat Heart* which was about men 'defeated in war, women in love'. She 'couldn't say' whether there was an implied eulogy for her marriage. Her sense of isolation was palpable, but there was also a softening towards her children. Of her poetry she said:

> What am I trying to achieve? The wholly selfish desire to write down something that is good. And if anybody asks me what makes poetry good, I say it is something you can feel in your bones and right through your brain – it's in your heart.

I spent three days with Sheila Wingfield. She gave her imprimatur for a biography I never wrote. But I did pen several pieces about her in the years that followed. Penny Perrick told me she found one wrapped around an antique bought in Galway and it piqued her interest in ultimately penning Sheila's story. I wrote about Sheila because I was aware of how much not being 'one of the male literary crowd' had played in her reputational positioning. In the late 1970s, I'd been forbidden to focus a PhD on Irish women writers. The adjudicator, a male don, declared he'd have 'none of that feminist bullshit'.

Sheila Wingfield seemed a totem of that lived experience in an Ireland steeped in gendered 'rules'. Classical archetypes and mythologies were a neutralising subversion of all that, making the personal global. Odysseus, as he dies, remembers not so much his adventures but his aging father digging in the garden – a scene that might have taken place in Eavan Boland's Dublin suburb even as it calls to heart the early death of Sheila's brother, Guy.

I continued writing to Sheila until she died in 1992. I also kept in contact with Eavan through RTÉ and various arts efforts. I suggested a television documentary to mark one of Eavan's birthdays. Then, in 2006, I pitched a proposal based on my personal recordings with Sheila Wingfield. I wanted to marry her life with her poetry and bring it to a new audience.

I phoned Eavan who said at once, 'Gosh, you've reminded me. Do you know I met her when I was eighteen? It was 1962 and I was a student working in a Dublin hotel.' Then, in another ripple that would vibrate across the years, Eavan revealed she too had once sat at the side of Sheila's bed, talking about verse to the first Irish woman poet she had ever met.

My documentary about Sheila, *Hiding in Plain Sight*, was broadcast on RTÉ TV in February 2007. In it Eavan re-champions Sheila as a writer just as she did with women in WEB/Arlen House courses – and as she continued to do for those who followed:

> Sheila Wingfield didn't have a place to put her foot in Ireland as an Irish poet. She deferred to a certain amount of the critical establishment and longed for their approval and felt she wouldn't get it and didn't have the wherewithal to stand up and push back. She came to the very threshold of the thing a poet needs, which is a very confirmed self, and some of her best poems are from that threshold. But she was an outsider, felt like an outsider, though perhaps didn't feel enough confidence to write like one.

After the documentary aired, Eavan published her essay 'A Latin Poet: A Lost Encounter' collected in *A Journey with Two Maps* (2011). She reiterated how Sheila Wingfield 'felt isolated' as a poet: 'Years later I realised [Sheila] had been talking about exclusions of gender as well as nation ... In the old nation, this woman in front of me had found no place.' Then a young, hopeful poet on her own threshold, Eavan 'shrank' from the gendered reality of Sheila's 'talk of disappointments ... inwardly I assured myself, whoever this was, I would never be like her.'

Yet the two writers shared so much, including their early appreciation of Yeats, an interest in Latin, the classics and imagery appropriated historically by male writers, which they attempted to make new. More fundamentally, they understood a 'straying sod' sense of disorientation in the wake of colonial displacements. Curiously, themes of home and impermanence appear in poems both women wrote about Powerscourt. In Eavan's case, the Dublin townhouse is captured through the prism of an Irish print discovered in a Chicago Museum, far from its Irish homeplace: 'naming the earth/seemed to me then/only a gateway to death.' ('On Seeing James Malton's Powerscourt House, Dublin 1795'). Whereas 'Sheila's View' (1974) marks the end of her Wicklow home: 'domes and domesticity, entire/As stallions, but now/Burnt to the ground'.

It's thirty-five years since those crucible months when I first met Eavan Boland and Sheila Wingfield. Thanks in part to their influences, I continue to write. I'm also vivified by documentary making: the marrying of visuals, sound and narrative with attempts at a kind of poetry. Much of that work, like *No Country For Women* (2018), relates to Irish women's place in history. But a documentary, like a poem, has its own canon of formats. Subject matter, authorship and permissions are too often mediated by those in power, not always wielded equally or wisely. In today's digital world, democratic routes mean many more have opportunities to be heard. Supporting and encouraging new voices is what I work towards. It's what Sheila Wingfield yearned for. It's what Eavan Boland helped a generation of women writers to achieve.

There are so many ways to pass the gifts of seeing and hearing forward. As Eavan said in *Hiding in Plain Sight*:

> We don't want the easy people, whose backgrounds we approve of or whose stories we recognise, to represent us as artists. We want the people who have a story to tell out of their humanity. We want to put aside our sense of race and

class and history and listen to those people. And Sheila Wingfield is one of them.

So too is Eavan Boland.

Poetry can ride some of the waves, washing away boundaries of equality, power, time and place. Perhaps by capturing a single image, possibly a classroom, a hospital or more simply an intimate domestic setting, a room where one woman helps another and is helped in return just by sitting, listening, opening hearts at the side of a bed on the threshold of change.

Susan Schreibman

My Heart Went Mad
for Ann Saddlemyer

Disturbed by her husband's mood on their honeymoon and
anxious to distract him from his brooding on Maud and Iseult
Gonne, she [George Yeats] had attempted a session of
automatic writing, only to discover a ready facility for that
spiritualist practice ...
Terence Brown, *The Life of W.B. Yeats*

On her honeymoon George used an old trick with a new
 twist
She called on the spirit world to reassure
A husband that he'd taken the right path
In a sacred wood her hand was grasped by another
As she swooned into other statedness
To interpret the voices of discarnate guides
They assured her husband that *with the bird all is well with
 the heart*
And that the cat and the hare moved in harmony
Long standing rheumatic pains, neuralgia, and fatigue
 receded
And his mind, previously unhinged by strain
Developed a clarity of vision
Mercury and Uranus joined bearing the gift of metaphor
And reassured him of the couple's future
Guiding a great mind, not into submission
But into acceptance, and maybe something called love

THE LAST HAT
for Hilary

The last hat
Belonging to the last member
Of the burial society remained
From the last village in Bohemia
To be evacuated
Before the black hand of death came

Three burial carts
From this village
On the river Elbe
Left behind one cold January day

The people who would have lain inside
This last enclosure for
Their last journey
To join the buried
In the cemetery of Brandýs nad Labem
Transported
Before the angel of death smote them

One Torah
Delivered to the Jewish museum in Prague
Labelled *1729*
With one red number
To facilitate its return
To the shtetl of 139 souls who loved it
Before the fires of hell incinerated them

Monica Strina

BLOOD MOON

Gaia is uncomfortable on the pebbles of the Nice seafront, between the Promenade des Anglais and what, here, passes for sea. She wishes she was on the shore of the Mediterranean, on the fine sand of the Poetto beach, lying beside the girl with whom she shared a night of falling stars in secondary school. As the moon fills with blood, Gaia looks at the palm of her hand, at a half-moon scar that is also on Flavia's palm. The cut of a Sardinian *Pattadese* knife. She opens Facebook on her phone, searches for a Flavia Martini. Finds twelve.

A wind starts snaking along the pebbles, lifting a white dust that in the heat sticks to her sweat like feathers on tar. This sea doesn't smell right, and neither does the skin of the man beside her. Gaia takes a notebook and a stick of charcoal out of her backpack and traces the curve of the moon twice, once in the sky, once on the sea. *Where are you?* She writes beside her drawing, and the side of her hand drags charcoal all over the page, printing the pattern of her skin again and again. Why not be afraid of a man's thick fingers; of curving your hand around the aggressive shape of his genitals? Why be terrified of brushing the gentler slope of a woman's? Mothers, she thinks, it has to do with mothers. She sees herself at twelve with a towel thick as a perch between her legs after a night of pain, and a woman who never warned her that she would bleed in the dark like a dying animal. Gaia stabs a pointy pebble onto the scar in her palm; drags it along until blood spurts out. A puny amount, nothing like what the pain has led her to believe. With her fingertips she spreads it on the first moon she has drawn, the one in the sky.

'What the hell are you doing?' says Marc. 'Can't you try to be normal?'

Guido has spent the night of 19 July dining at The Scotsman for the last forty years. Always the window seat, always the candle, and always a red sweater, like on the night of Adar's twenty-second birthday, only this time the moon's beauty is helping him forget that she won't come.

After dinner, he will make his way downstairs to the old-fashioned cinema, where he'll be served ice cream – chocolate, but strawberry for her, if she were here – and sink into a leather seat, and watch a black-and-white movie, something like *Arsenic and Old Lace* or the original *Sabrina*. *To Kill a Mockingbird*, on the night she had been here. Then he will climb up the stairs, more and more slowly each year, spend the night in a cheaper hotel, remembering, and fly back to Florence.

They were students then, but her father had let her use his credit card for a birthday dinner. Guido's present had been a thin silver band, which sparkled against her dark skin. There were tears on it.

'I'll be here. On this day. Till you come back.'

'My parents have arranged the marriage, Guido. I can't –'

'19 July, The Scotsman. Adar! Just don't forget.'

Those words, her face framed in candlelight, the shine in her black hair, the shimmer of her nose ring are as vivid as the present, yet each year past hurts now in the manner of a bruise. Does the moon look the same in Mumbai?

Filippo is on the terrace of a beach house, holding his little girl whose head is boiling through his shirt, heavy with a sleep which depth he envies. But this makes him think of death, so he squeezes his eyes shut and visualises stone blocks forming the word 'NEVER', three times, then wonders whether he has turned off the tap in the bathroom, and if so did he tighten it so much it will break? His wife won't be happy. She has caught him in the act of throwing away the first bit of toothpaste before using it – the part that has touched someone else's toothbrush. She has noticed the raw skin on the backs of his hands, minced-meat skin, from too much soap and too much washing. And all the times when he hurries out of a room to repeat his mantras somewhere he won't be seen or heard. If she leaves, will she use all of this to gain custody?

Filippo lowers himself on a deck chair, the girl's hair tickling his chin, redolent of sweat and green apple. The moon has changed from a doubloon into a wound, and reminds him of the stigmata on the crucifix that hung in the parochial hall when he was a child. He could hardly look at it. Sitting at Catechism, he had thought he was good – well, he was all right – till the parish priest had told him otherwise. Filippo realised then that he had wasted time thinking about video games and football rather than working to save himself from the eternal flames. He discovered dangers he had never known – a sin that was unforgivable. What if he went and did it? What if thinking about it so much made him do it; what if thinking about it not at all meant he would forget and do it by mistake?

His daughter shivers in the first breath of a mistral wind, scented with myrtle berry and sea spray. Her heart and his are beating out of time with each other, composing a tune-deaf melody he reads as a bad omen.

'I wish I could show you how beautiful it all is,' he whispers, caressing her curls, 'but when I try, all that comes out is blood.'

Pablo can't see the moon, because he can't touch it. What he can see is his girlfriend's hand, her fingers woven through his as they sit with their backs against a mahogany tree; he can see the leg that's touching his, and her face, too, not because it is lying on his shoulder, but because it usually is. Pablo wears sunglasses to hide his eyes; he doesn't know that Treasure Beach is reflected on their lenses, its palm trees turned black, the sky drained and cold blue.

And the moon.

'The moon,' says Grace, 'is different from any other night. It's like copper, it's ... like someone got bored of white, and painted it the most startling colour. Like you stretched your hand to grab something you believed to be cold and burnt your skin.'

Her voice too is visible, a ribbon of smooth fabric that brushes against his face. A crab surfaces from its hole in the sand, headbutts Pablo's bare foot, then plunges back in. What if the colour of the moon confuses the turtles that lay their eggs on the shores of Barbados, and they refuse to let their offspring fall onto the damp sand?

'You always know how to make me see,' he says into the palm of Grace's hand, but she, too, is a different colour tonight. Is it the moon, calling to her blood? Pablo has often felt a tidal quality in women, the pull of something stronger than any man.

The sea is full of whispers tonight, distracted in a game with the poisonous fruits of the manchineel tree; the song of the frogs fills every silence, vibrating so loudly it makes the darkness throb.

'Ssh,' says the sea, 'ssh,' and Pablo thinks he should obey; he knows he should let it go.

'You are leaving me,' he says.

Grace's tears glisten in the lenses of his sunglasses, but he only sees them when he smells salt. When they fall like acid rain on the back of his hand.

Danny sits on the parapet of the River Liffey, just before it meets the Ha'penny Bridge. He looks at the city lights, O'Connell Bridge, the Spire, the GPO. He looks at his own clothes, an ironed shirt, suit pants with the crease in the right place, and pointy shoes, quite shiny still, and wonders why all this, and having a wife and a boy waiting for him at home, and yes, a home – he wonders why all this does not *feel* like anything. It's like words on the side of a passing bus. When Jaime was in the womb, Danny thought he knew him and loved him already; but the moment he came out looking different from what Danny expected, looking angry, looking pained, Danny felt as though he was a stranger, someone he might not want to know – and suddenly, his wife – she, too, turned into someone detached from him, whose skin did not need his; whose eyes no longer softened when he talked to her. A different light started shining on the memories of their relationship, uncovering all kinds of *things* – and who is holding up that torch, now; who's moving it around, picking out all those grimy, cobwebbed corners littered with corpses? How does one make it stop?

But it isn't work and it isn't her and it isn't the baby and it isn't the Dublin weather. People say hey, he killed himself because his girlfriend left him; she killed herself because she was fired from her job, but that's like saying you got cancer because you ate red meat.

Danny looks at the black water of the Liffey with the tops of bicycle wheels, traffic cones and umbrellas breaking through the surface and sees a deep red hole. Its edges tremble in the wind like those of a bed sheet, and he remembers the first girl he was with, her blood all over the bed, too much of it so that they'd both been scared, but it had been ok, all of it except the sheet that had been ruined. Is she watching this same moon, he wonders – the one he can only look at in dirty water, his eyes too weighed-down to climb up to the sky? Would he be sitting here, pushing himself closer and closer to the slippery edge of the parapet, if he had stayed with her?

Tina is sitting on the grass beside a grave in Southampton's Old Cemetery. It's her favourite, the one with the headstone that tells the story of an eighteen-year-old boy out with his friends having fun, hiding from a storm under a tree, meeting with a bolt of lightning. There are always tea lights on this grave, their flames dancing as though he is wiggling his fingers down there, jittering the way teenagers do. She leans her head against the headstone and venerates the moon.

Tina is alone and she probably shouldn't be here: she's a girl, after all, but she's only been one for the last two months, and she has spent them recovering from the operation. There is something moving in the long grass, and someone has placed a daffodil into the hand of a stone angel, a sexless being so beautiful it makes her want to cry. There is a vulnerability to being a woman – physically – that she had considered before, but never felt, and it is a thing of fear and beauty. She feels like a landscape from which a row of ugly buildings has been removed.

'I'm scared,' she tells the moon.

The bushes beside her open, and the largest rat she has ever seen waddles out. Tina scrambles to her feet but the rat ignores her, and after sniffing around scuttles back into the shadows, its pink-grey paws almost cute under its lumbering body. Tina sits down again and tries to imagine it returning to a family of baby rats to take care of them, hiding from people who wouldn't mind squashing it.

Raymond collapses on the ground in Place de la Contrescarpe, but manages to hurt only his bottom. Or the bones sticking out of the hollow where his bottom once was. People look away. He would do the same. But he's made it. He's seen once more the second-hand bookshops, a treat he used to allow himself on Saturdays; the restaurants with the blackboards saying *volaille* and *coq au vin* and *avec ses pommes de terre*, the air freckled with darkness. At the hospice they will be looking for him, worrying about the morphine leaving his bloodstream, the bundle of bones tied to one another his body has become. Ah, what a moon. Is this punishment, he wonders, and if so, why then is everything so beautiful? As pain reaches its tendrils to his stomach, he steals the red moon and hides it at the bottom of his eyes; he breathes in the summer air so that what isn't a black mass of deranged cells inside him is – becomes – the air of his last day in Paris.

Flavia doesn't know about the moon, but she sees red, too – on the inside of her thighs, smudged, all the way down to her knees. It's on their double bed, the one they have shared since they got married. She despises this bed. The things it knows; the things it says when it creaks. She puts a bloody handprint on the coverlet, then hobbles to the utility room and picks up a hammer. It hurts to walk. With both hands she brings the hammer down onto the headboard. It sounds like bones.

Crack, crack, goes the wood, splintering, showing its real colour hidden on the inside.

They won't listen. They won't believe her. He will say you know what she's like, she'd say no all the time if you let her, and can you even rape your own wife?

But it hasn't started today. It began on the afternoon when her father came back from work early and found her with the girl from the grocery store down the road. His hands were mallets. She thought they would sever her limbs. But the way he sat down afterwards, and put his face in his hands, and cried!

Flavia was sent to a Christian community where everyone was always smiling and talking of forgiveness, and where an older lady introduced her to her son. Her dad gave her away at the wedding.

She thinks of the pills. She bought them weeks ago, counted them, poured them all into the same bottle. Should she write a letter to say goodbye? But to whom?

She takes a scalding shower to wash him off. It stings like fucking jellyfish. She imagines flaying herself, so that no cell he has touched is left. Then she takes a backpack and throws in a change of clothes, her wallet and her *Pattadese* knife, her mobile phone. She doesn't take the house keys. She does take the bottle of pills.

Outside, the air is liquid with humidity. She finds a rock and throws it at the kitchen window, which shatters with a musical sound.

'Madam, are you ok?' It's a boy, maybe seventeen, the age she was when she fell in love with a girl on the Poetto beach, gazing at a shower of stars. She could slap him for calling her madam. 'You ...' He points at her trousers, and she sees it. More red.

In the ambulance they find the pills and look at her but she turns away. She begs them not to take the knife. She looks at the half-moon cut on the palm of her right hand, and wishes all this blood was coming from there.

The girl who's fixing her IV line is younger than she is and visibly competent. Flavia wonders when it was that all the people she admires – actresses, medical staff, musicians – went from being a lot older than she was to being suddenly, irremediably, younger.

'Some moon, mh?' the girl says to her colleague, who's taking down Flavia's details.

Flavia's phone beeps and the man hands it to her. The message is from Salvatore.

'Please,' she says. 'Please, throw it out of the window.'

The paramedics give each other a look.

'What? We can't ...' the man says, then the phone beeps again.

Flavia looks at the screen. There is a number 1 on the icon of her Facebook app. But her eyelids are growing heavy, pain claiming every corner of her body.

The woman hurries out of the taxi, then just stands on the kerb, hands on her stomach, the tiredness of the trip weighing on her limbs like a cold. A ring flashes silver against the bodice of her mauve sari, held up by a necklace. The town hurts her with a beauty she has missed; reminds her of winter evenings spent running from one café to the next in an attempt to warm herself, ordering a hot chocolate in each one, borrowing time.

Her grown-up sons rang her while she was in the taxi, their voices worried and sceptical – she has never travelled without their father, and now he's gone they think she should travel only with them.

She lets her legs take her to the places they know, the roads that were as solid in her dreams as they now are under her shoes. If anyone knew why she came, they would think her senile; but she will never tell. She will hail another taxi to the airport, return to India, and this time she will be at peace knowing there is no snapped thread blowing in the wind, waiting for her to tie it back to herself.

She only sees the moon once she is standing before The Scotsman. She sees it reflected on the window, and inside its red circle is the face of the boy with whom the girl she used to be, has spent, in secret, the last forty years.

Breda Wall Ryan

HERITAGE

Children kick through fairy fog
where summer sun burns off the dew,
reminding me of a long-gone field
hand-sown with *Fescue, Cocksfoot,*
Timothy, Rye, Common Bent, Foxtail,
dry-mixed in a galvanised bucket,
as a home baker combines
wholemeal, sifted white, oatmeal,
salt and soda to her secret recipe.

Each field, broadcast, trodden and rolled
differed from the neighbour's as each
farmwife's loaf had its own texture and savour.
Meadow and loaf held their secrets close: ratio,
number of handfuls, size of measuring hand.
The meadow was once a speckled tweed
of purples, yellows, greens and blues,
good grazing for ancient cattle breeds,
Droimeann, Kerry, Dexter and Moiled polly,
pedigrees stretching back to the *Bó Cúailgne.*

The baker brings forth her perfect loaf
of close-grained wholemeal bread
slathered with butter to nourish
grandchildren tumbling through fairy fog.

And what will these children remember?
Only the fog, the bread, their excited running?
Or Grandmother's talk of *Daisy, Self Heal,*
Lady's Smock, Clover, Meadowsweet,
Sorrel, Yarrow, the vanished pink smoke
of flowering grasses?

WE ARE OCEAN

We are ocean, all of us. Ocean
where Salmon and Dolphin once leapt,
gulping clean air above waves that tumbled
one over another, as they should;

where Dolphin's shining teeth snatched
Salmon mid-air, muscled him down his throat,
one life giving life to another,
exchanging molecules, as they should.

How does it feel to be dead?

Living our small lives, we come to the shore.
Fearing Earth's reprisal, an exchange
of zoonotic burdens, we keep our distance
one from another. We are ocean.

Our town elders knew, added Mermaid
to our coat of arms; also Martelet, bird
without feet, condemned to endless flight
in pursuit of knowledge. Knowledge we ignore,

to our peril. There is nothing here to save us;
No Dolphin, nor Salmon; no Mermaid
nor mythic legless bird. Swallows swoop
in endless pursuit of insects,

molecules change places. Waves tumble
seaglass, grind it back to sand.
Two mallards fly past a rainbow.
The rainbow dissolves in dark cloud.

Ocean, how will it feel to be dead?

DUSK

Fuchsia bells drip nectar,
bees fly hiveward in thinned light.

Bats in meagre skies
hoover up moths and midges.

I remember bright buttercup, dandelion,
cuckoo pint, sweet clover, vetch and trefoil;
poppy and rosebay willow for mellow mood.

This was my favourite field.
And now?

Rooks tear out divots, feast on leatherjackets.
Pheasants roost in alder, above nightfox reach.
Hedgehogs crunch snails by the compost heap.

The ride-on mower tames wild grasses to lawn.
A John Deere rumbles past, scalping August hedges.
Lights startle small birds into song.

Snarls of motorway traffic trouble the dusk.
A hidden landfill reeks of decay.

Outside of memory,
can the meadow survive?

Dolores Walshe

THIS HAMLET

I've ruined things with the guy I fancy, thanks to Ma. Sometimes I feel like I'm her wound.

Once, for homework, Maggie and I used fridge magnets to test her da Richie's key to the banger of a car he had to pay to get towed away. But there was no attraction. We knew then the key was brass, an alloy of copper and zinc.

I wish Richie was my da too, but what I have is this internet one. Since Monday, when Ma finally broke her silence.

He did a runner when he found out she was pregnant. I'm scared there's something even darker under this.

Think metaphor, Binchy says in English Lit; well this week vomit's mine.

No Twitter account, a website you can't leave a message on but there're details of his dodgy life: married for five minutes divorced, married ditto, in a relationship no longer in one, beautiful women slick as seals leaning in to him, actors directors, an orthopaedic doctor.

Well she didn't fix him, that's for sure.

No kids. *That you know of,* a talk-show host in America jokes to him on YouTube but he doesn't crack a lip, just veers off on another topic; deflection, Binchy calls this.

Once Ma got mugged wheeling home her flower stall. The mugger smashed her nose with a toy mallet, took her cashbox while she lay half-dazed on the pavement wondering if the mallet belonged to his child, how he'd explain her blood to the kid.

He took all the notes but threw the small change at her. This is the most detailed story I know about Ma. When the hospital fixed her up, she rushed home, worried at being late picking me up from Maggie's ma, Sandra, who was minding me for the first time. She says I stood in my little pink dress staring up at the white bandage on her nose, saying Old Smokey, Mama.

I don't remember this. It's Ma's memory given to me as my own, which makes it more important than any of mine because someday she'll die and leave me; all I'll have are these pictures that help me remember she never abandoned me.

The parking attendant tried to charge her for her stall in the hospital car park but, seeing her snow-capped nose, he patted her arm and said it's ok love. Then he walked away. This part always gets me crying because someone actually *saw* Ma. He was my first father because of this, not that he'll ever know.

There were tulips scattered on the wet pavement and in the gutter beside Ma, as if they'd crawled there seeking moisture to prolong themselves. These were the cracked-stemmed broken-petalled bent-backed ones she couldn't sell, being brought home to our house to be placed in jam jars where the sun'd catch them and they'd try to straighten themselves for one last glimpse of the world.

That night she put me in the bath to teach me to swim. She doesn't know why. She kept this up for a week even though the hot water cost. But when she took me to the swimming pool I screamed my head off for my little soapy sea. The lifeguard told her to stop terrorising me and Ma said if that was the case my face would look like her nose. But she gave up after that, gave up selling flowers too, started cleaning offices instead. The stall got hail rain and snowed on in our tiny backyard. One of the frostiest Christmases it got so crystallised it held me hypnotised at the window till I almost froze too. We smashed it one of the times we ran out of gas. As the wood burnt we swore we could smell every flower it'd held, as if their essences had climbed inside the grain expecting safety and instead found themselves conducting heat.

Metal's another conductor of heat. When Richie goes into his darkness gripping the car key as if he thinks he'll be able to drive back out of it quick, we can't believe how hot he makes it. Sandra often forces it out of his hand, balances it back on top of their fat honeymoon candle that's never been lit on the mantelpiece, where he can see it when he returns. It's there now when Maggie and I walk in, gleaming in the sun like it's a beacon winking hard to draw him back to where he belongs.

But he's seated on the couch, staring out the window at the row of terraced houses facing ours that he calls the opposing army.

He's big and beautiful and mountain-still, eyes flickering at the movie in his head.

Sandra says she's no idea where his mind goes so we've stopped asking her, though we know she's lying. He hasn't moved since we left for school this morning, long elegant fingers still draping the threadbare patch on the couch arm. The worst of days then. Sunlight on his face too, but what he's seeing isn't in the room. We each kiss a cheek, hoping he'll laugh. He barely nods. There'll be no interest in our homework so, there's been none for days. We clasp hands, silenced.

Sandra must've forced the key from him just before we got in because his other hand's got a groove cutting across his lifeline where the metal's bitten, as if making the forward thrust of his days uncertain. She walks in now, looks at him, sighs, tells us to study upstairs. We gather our school bags, glad to escape.

Maggie's room throbs with summer heat. We haul off school jumpers, fling them. She kicks off her shoes, looks at me. I stiffen, saying nothing, and go on the computer, checking *him* again. But I'm watching her sideways, hoping she will, hoping she won't. She toes one of the free posters from under the bed. It rolls away across the floor, then, as if it's hit a force field, rolls swiftly back. We've avoided it for days. Our breaths speed up. I tighten my arms across my chest, holding my heart in. Finally she nudges the poster with her toe, giving me another look, the black arch of her right eyebrow higher than her left. I fix my eyes on it, nails foraging under my blouse, digging into upper-arm flesh, wanting to bury themselves. The poster crackles as she unrolls it. There's a glimpse of him before it spools back up. She unspools it again, pins the four corners with science, math, history, biology.

We stare down at him on the poster, not speaking, so boggled and angry over him and saddened over Richie in our minds.

There's nothing of me in him, I'm reddish-skinned, all Ma. I close my eyes. But he's inside: anguished handsome face, loose cream shirt, his doublet and hose. I want to throw up over fancying him before I knew.

He took the boat to England right after he got Ma pregnant. Some fucking irony, him rubbing elbows with all those women forced to sneak across the sea for an abortion; I hope the ones with morning sickness threw up all over him.

I say *got* because Ma said it with an emphasis that terrified me. Who is it I'm sharing genes with? I took Ma saying *got* out on Johnny Harlow, punched him in the face when he slipped his hand up to unhook my bra, even though we'd been sucking the faces off each other, even though it was what I most wanted him to do.

They met at a dance. We know this from eavesdropping when Ma talks to Sandra.

Which is gazillions right now.

It was us bringing home the posters last Monday that broke Ma's silence. Was this what she gave the money for, *this* Hamlet? All bristles and stutters. Yeah, we said, sure we told you, he's in the Royal Shakespeare, our class is booked to go this Saturday night.

Thinking she was short, eejit me told her I'd walk to the theatre and back and Maggie said she'd walk too, run a marathon just to see drop-dead gorgeous Alex Sherwood in the flesh, and cool we didn't have to wear our uniforms, didn't need supervision to make our way there and back.

Only not Alex Sherwood. Michael Doyle, Ma squawked. Yeah, we knew, sure we'd read the Wikipedia entry on him. Still, she surprised us, she can barely send a text.

Then Ma the volcano: words spewing into the air, exploding with threats of what she'd do to him before she scarpered next door away from my face, from the lava ripping through my chest.

Is that me in the sideboard mirror, I asked Maggie in a weird voice. She said yes, I hadn't vacated myself. I liked the way she was talking, her arms a vice around me. Gradually I stopped trembling. We sneaked in then after Ma and sat on the stairs, hearing her blubbering it all to Sandra in the kitchen.

Then, silence. Then Ma crying, the midnight keening of an animal in pain from when I was small, splitting me open.

Then the hall door pushing in.

Richie. Risen from his doldrums, dark eyes shining into our upset, this beautiful man who wasn't my father.

The Jedi, Maggie said, dragging me upright. He held out his arms. We crashed into his chest so hard he hissed, rocking on his feet.

Ma told you, didn't she, Maggie said, she rang you at the factory and told you.

He drew us to sit in the living room. We sat in his arms, my head on his chest, his heart pumping into my pulse till finally it kept time with his. He pointed at our schoolbooks on the table.

Pick one, he said to Maggie, but not *Hamlet*, let's forget him for now. She picked Solzhenitsyn's stories. He opened it. Let's take our minds off our woes, he said. But he scanned some lines on a page, knuckled his eyes and sighed.

We sat up straight.

What? Maggie said, picking up the book. What, Da? Richie didn't answer, just leaned back against the couch, staring into space. Maggie peered at the page then started reading about a man who threw a log onto a fire before realising it was covered in ants. He pulled the burning log off so they could escape onto the ground. But they didn't run away. They turned and circled their 'forsaken homeland' and loads of them climbed back onto the burning log.

Maggie put the book down. Richie's eyelids were drawn like shutters. We cried with the pain of him gone again. Out in the hall our mas whispered, heading to the pub.

The auditorium's packed and he's making the stage blaze, sweating and spittling, striding about playing at sadness, madness, at missing his da.

Maggie whispers at me to stop grinding my teeth then seethes in my ear he's just a straightforward prick too cowardly to take responsibility. Everyone's reciting his soliloquies around us.

He's all the words Binchy called him in class; tortured, heart-sore, conflicted, cruel to his mother and his girlfriend, Ophelia, but we're sure none of this is true of him in real life, except the cruelty.

Ma begged me not to come tonight, afraid I'd be charmed by the man who told her someone else must be the father. I stare at this arsehole dragging his pretend grief around Elsinore. Jesus Christ, Ma, as *if*.

Earlier this evening all dolled up I'd climbed carefully through the gap in the broken fence to Richie building a barbeque in his backyard with bricks from the vacant lot, Sandra threatening to leave him if he didn't busy himself.

He'd called me darlin', an arm around my shoulder, asking was I sure I wanted to see this man. One time Maggie screamed at Richie that he was only half a da, good at going missing from himself. He'd stood, silent, pain blading his face. Then he'd said it was for her he always came back, his voice so quiet it made me sick with longing.

Thinking about this I started to cry and pulled away from him to stop my make-up mussing his shirt. Maggie came out then, distracting us. She's never needed make-up, not with Richie's big eyes, ropes of black hair glittering over one shoulder.

A paper plane whizzes now between the two of us, strikes the back of the red velvet seat in front. From Johnny Harlow. 'Bitch' it says. Maggie crushes it.

We go back to watching the stage.

When he walks about in his stockings saying *to be or not to be* the girls howl. The boys yawn. We sneak vodka from our plastic bottles. At the interval we guzzle the rest in the toilets. It pulses in me all through the next act, through Fortinbras getting his men to lift this sperm donor playing at dead, carry him off, vanquished at last.

The place erupts in a screaming ovation and outside there's headlights, traffic, pushing and shoving in the stampede for the stage door.

He's last to come out, smiling in a cone of streetlight as he signs autographs, us hanging back at the end of the line, vodka'd up.

I'm numb by the time we get to him, just us, nobody behind. He's tired now of adoration, poster smile spooled up for the night.

Saving the best for last, he murmurs, skimming past my pastiness, gaze travelling Maggie's face, taking in her beauty. For the first time I'm glad I'm average.

Maggie holds her programme out. It's quivering. He'll take this as proof-positive of his heart-throb status, wings of dark hair swept back from a sunbed tan as he signs his stage name: *To Maggie, thanks for coming xx.*

And you, young lady? Hand outstretched. What's your name, love?

Love. Oh boy.

It's so hard to look at him, but I hold it out, my programme trembling worse than Maggie's. It's for my mother, I manage.

He regards me properly finally, a searching look, something behind it making me feel uneasy. Yet another groupie too shy to ask for his autograph, that what he's thinking?

I say Ma's full name.

There's no change of expression. He scrawls the words at speed, as if he wants rid of us, Ma dead to him, me too.

Handing me back the programme, he asks quietly if I'd like my name on it too. I shake my head hard.

So it's *really* your mother who wants it, he mutters.

And up it comes: fury unleashed. Yes, I say, really, I suppose for my ma one time long ago that was true but if he was signing for *me* he'd have to stop acting the maggot and use his *real* fucking name.

A pause of theatrical proportions: oh the irony of this, top marks from Binchy for sure.

Traffic passing, the swish of a tram, me rattling, Maggie's hand crushing mine, him looking down at leather-shod feet, no way out of this street.

Yes, he whispers, half-strangled, raising his head. Those flawlessly carved lips clap then, a sad little castanet.

Yes what? I screech it, what does *yes* mean, you can't even ad lib, what sort of ham actor are you anyway? And stop mouthpiecing Hamlet, just think what a piece of work *you* are, raping my mother!

Maggie gasps, jerking me away. We turn swiftly, leaving him there on the pavement, stumbling off fast as we can into the lit dark, heading for the river. Maggie glances back as we're rounding the corner.

Jesus, Evie, she squeaks, he's still standing there with his hand out!

We cross the bridge, Maggie keeping watch while I lean over, emptying my guts into the water below.

We take forever then dragging home, silent, completely wrecked, Maggie spraying us with perfume when we get to our street. A taxi passes, stopping further along. The car door opens and he's there, striding towards us, Hamlet, all doubt gone, terrifying us.

Maggie gets her door open. We're shoving into the hall, squealing, as he catches my arm, saying how could I accuse him of that!

Then Ma and Sandra, pushing him away from me, him saying stuff about Instagram and Facebook, Ma calling him a wanker.

Richie, I wail, and he lunges through the living room door at Alex Sherwood, the key gripped in his palm, the blow bursting through the movie in his head as if it must.

Jesus, Ma says, shaky as hell, I think you've broken his nose.

Well, Richie says grimly, hauling him up off the floor, a nose for a nose.

The hall's stuffed with heaving breaths, then silence for a bit.

Are ... y'alright, Ma says then. She gestures vaguely into the air as if conjuring a rabbit. I suppose you'd ... better sit?

I stare at her, at Alex Sherwood collapsing with a grunt on the stairs, an Everest peaking on his face. Then I'm running, ashamed, outside through the yard, through the gap in the fence to my house, I can't get upstairs fast enough to lock myself in.

I lie for hours, through Maggie knocking, then Ma, the duvet pulled over my head. When all goes quiet, I toss it back. It's still dark, cigarette smoke drifting in the window.

Richie. Below in his yard, the glow lighting his face, all molten as he inhales. I lean out the window. The air's still warm.

A siren sounds somewhere. A cat miaows. Then, among the geyser burst of beer cans opening, the new nasal strangeness of his voice alongside Richie's.

I lean further out, peering at their shapes.

Even then, Richie's saying, yes even then, something something-something left him unspeakably alone. And by *unspeakably* he means he stopped speaking then.

Richie talking as he never has, as if some new alloy is forming, Alex Sherwood murmuring in response, nasal, drawn-out, as if gladder to be here than in some emergency room awaiting X-ray results.

Máiríde Woods

THE AUNT'S STORY

This story is based on true events. Part of my aunt's interview with one of her father's killers was cited in Peter Hart's book The IRA and its Enemies *(OUP, 1999). I have changed the names of the people my aunt met during her search.*

I sit with her notebook on my lap, retrieved from my sister's belongings. Beige, student-style, narrow feint – I owned several myself, filled with notes, quotations, doodles. Hers holds an account of her quest for answers to her father's death. She had the sort of purpose I lack.

It's many years since I've seen this notebook. My Aunt Marie is nearly forty years dead after a way of life now considered odd and unfashionable. She writes in a round, clear script. Fountain pen, no biro. Some pages contain my own father's disjointed handwriting. He started the search and they shared information, possibly through this notebook. Marie was the one who succeeded in finding answers, who sat opposite one of the men responsible.

My grandfather, James O'Donoghue, was an RIC man who joined the constabulary in the 1890s. A native Irish speaker from Kerry, he was the eldest son in a large family and decided against the farm. Three of his sisters emigrated to the USA and helped educate younger siblings. By his mid-forties, James was a sergeant in Cork. In mid-November 1920, as he walked to his barracks, three men shot him in White Street. He was unarmed. The same night a number of young men from nearby were shot – almost certainly in a reprisal raid. The IRA command later sent an apology to James's family, but at the time of the funeral, no undertaker in the city would provide a hearse, because of IRA threats. After several failed attempts, James's brother, Father Michael got a car from Waterville to move the coffin.

My grandmother Margaret never recovered – despite returning to Dublin, her home town, where her brother Bill and his family lived. She turned to alcohol and died four years later. Before her death, Uncle Michael became guardian to the two children, thirteen and ten at the time of their father's killing. They were sent to boarding schools, spending their holidays with two of the O'Donoghue aunts who had returned to Kerry from America. Their uncle got them to promise to remain silent about their father's death and eschew any revenge.

I turn the pages of the notebook. To begin with there are news accounts copied from the *Cork Examiner*, *The Irish Times*, the *Independent*, along with expressions of outrage from editors and bishops. There was no photocopying when my father found them first; I imagine him in the National Library transcribing the gruesome details of bullet holes, the cap that rolled away, the committee of enquiry report. It's a story I've known in outline since I was eleven, but I've felt unequal to writing it. I've lived a quietish life, leaving Northern Ireland before the Troubles erupted, suffering only common-or-garden buffetings of fortune. It has been the type of life my father and aunt wanted for me and my sisters, part of the reason they kept their childhood sealed off. When we visited our aunt's convent, we knew we should present the picture of a happy childhood with polite recitations and games. The talk was mainly of schools – hers and ours. She and the other nuns went to great lengths to keep us amused, though we remained slightly in awe of her judgements, some showing a strong moral sense, others infected with snobbery.

Marie joined a semi-enclosed order with continental connections. My father married and became a teacher in Northern Ireland; her subject was Irish, his history. Both of them had enormous respect for their Uncle Michael and felt bound by the promise they had made him. Yet my father too had sought information about his father's death. As well as trawling the newspaper accounts, he visited the scene in White Street, and located the graves of those killed in the reprisal raids – according to an ex-RIC man, one was a suspect. But his attempts to find more information failed.

The Vatican Council was instrumental in Marie's search. It opened up life for nuns. By the mid-1960s they were less restricted, were allowed more personal belongings and more frequent letters. They could travel alone for courses and to visit relatives. The sacrifice the earlier enclosure rules entailed is obvious in a story Marie told of an occasion when she had to pass the home of her ailing Kerry aunts without visiting. 'It broke my heart,' she said. 'Why didn't you resist?' I almost asked. But I knew the answer: subjecting your will to the rule was part of the nun's 'vocation'.

The years of sacrifice erased neither her memories nor her strong will. By the time the opportunity to seek answers arose, she was over sixty. 'There was a car going to Cork,' the first sentence of her account reads, 'and I asked them to drop me at Patrick Street.' What did she tell them, I wonder? Her companions seemed unaware of her early life. Her only confidant was my father – but she did not reveal these expeditions to him until afterwards. As he had, she started with businesses near the yard in White Street, seeking an old person who might remember November 1920. Her cover story was that she was teacher doing research on that period. To her surprise several people did remember – and she was comforted by those who said that the sergeant was a good man, who had been shot in error.

Although I remember my father speaking of how Marie had met one of the gunmen – and his reaction of admiration and envy at her investigative skills – it was the early eighties before I got a fuller picture. By then my parents were dead. My father had enjoined us to 'look after Marie' and we would visit and invite her for short stays in Dublin. Although she delighted in seeing us and our children, I sometimes felt that outside her convent she looked a bit lost. During one of her visits she began – deliberately, I think – talking of her past.

In the notebook she starts with her memories of the night her father was killed. She describes her upset at having arrived home too late to accompany him to the barracks.

'It had been a practice of mine owing to dangerous times – but my father disliked it and only agreed because it relieved mother's anxiety,' she writes.

That evening, after missing his departure, she heard the shots and reached White Street, only to see an ambulance departing. She then walked on her own to the Union Quay

Barracks with the awful feeling that it was her father who had been shot.

As a thirteen-year-old she took on a lot of responsibility. Months later, it was she who persuaded her mother to return to Dublin, though the child in her told us how much she regretted having to leave her dolls behind. They stayed first with Margaret's brother, Bill, later finding a house in Drumcondra. In 1922, during the Civil War, Marie went on a holiday to her Kerry aunts. This turned into a stay of several months when the railway line was cut. On her return to Dublin she was shocked by her mother's deterioration and by my father's truanting. She decided to write to Uncle Michael. He came to Dublin, where he insisted on becoming guardian to both children. Perhaps it was a necessary move, but it was a betrayal of her mother. I did wonder if it influenced her decision to enter the convent, if she had made a sort of bargain with God. In that era Catholics would worry about whether a person had died 'in a state of grace' – particularly when a death was sudden. God was real and important in people's lives and certainly in hers.

At her boarding school, the nuns treated her with kindness and theirs was the order she entered after taking her degree. She ended up as principal in one of their schools. Her passionate nature and sense of drama made her an excellent teacher and, despite her tiny stature, she never had any discipline problems. She wasn't easily intimidated – I remember her chasing apple thieves out of the convent orchard. She was a devoted Gaeilgeoir; on childhood visits in our new summer dresses, we would parrot Irish phrases and songs to create the impression we had some Irish. I fear we were a disappointment!

Several times I started writing this story but stopped. Was it mine to tell? Though I deeply regret both my grandparents' deaths, for me they were Edwardian figures from a wedding photo in a curlicued frame. It seemed inauthentic to flesh out Marie's account with my (late twentieth-century) imagination. There were so many gaps.

As a child in the North, I had been an unthinking nationalist, only later committing to non-violence. I was in Dublin during the 1966 commemoration of the Rising, a less nuanced event than the recent centenary. I remember feeling an ambivalence about my RIC connection, though my grandfather was known for 'being good to the boys'. In earlier decades my father and aunt must have felt far more ambivalence, surrounded as they were by conflicting loyalties. Not only had their father been in the RIC, but their mother's brother had worked for Collins. In 1921, shortly after they moved to Dublin, Uncle Bill's life was actually saved, when Black and Tans raiding his home discovered James's RIC uniform and withdrew. Despite having hard words for republicans, my father stayed in touch all his life with his mother's family. Both he and Marie put greater emphasis on personal conscience and responsibility than is the fashion today. Systemic failure had not been invented. Yet there must have been difficult silences and bitten-back words.

My early attempt to tell this story took the perspective of a young person who thought, with the unconscious arrogance of the 1960s generation, that people needed to leave the past behind. And yet I knew how contradictory the past is, how it sticks around, even when shown the door. My father and Marie's faithfulness to their father's memory impressed me, and I sensed the broken nature of their relationship with a mother who was also a victim and whom I resembled. They seldom mentioned her, impatient I think, with her inability to put her children before her grief and addiction. Would I have done any better?

So I'm back with the notebook. First Marie's account of the night of the killing: the sound of the shots, the Angelus bell, which she recalled but which didn't fit the time frame established later, her walk to the barracks, her meeting with a friend who said it was her father who had been shot. Then her mother's plea for no reprisals, their all-night prayers, the funeral Mass in St Finbarr's, the coffin roped onto the car from Kerry. The bleakness of that day.

Later pages detail her visits to Cork between 1968 and 1973. Each time she returns to White Street as to a shrine. She notes the impression she makes as a nun entering a pub (once an IRA headquarters) and a barber's shop. The four elderly men she speaks to confirm there had been three gunmen waiting near the yard that night.

'I was amazed at how clearly each recalled the event – without thought or hesitation,' she writes. On that first visit in late October, she recalls her father's last Hallowe'en: she had brought barmbrack to his barracks; he had helped her with her sums.

A casual piece of information brings her to the hardware shop, owned, she believes, by one of the gunmen, Lawrence. He is absent – in hospital. When she explains her 'research', his son sends her down the familiar streets to meet his aunt.

She knocks on Aunt Kathleen's door. Kathleen had been the wife of a man killed in the 1920 reprisal raid. She later married another from 'the movement', who, Marie suspects, was also one of the gunmen. He is many years dead. In 1920 they all lived barely a stone's throw from the O'Donoghues. Marie describes her as 'in her seventies very alert, very sharp, and very worn and old for her age'. Kathleen offers to lend Marie news cuttings about the events of 1920–21 and recounts how the yard in White Street was used to store guns brought in by ship from Germany. Slowly the conversation moves towards the night of Sergeant O'Donoghue's death. Kathleen indirectly confirms Marie's suspicions as to the identity of the three gunmen. Two are dead, the third seems to be her brother Lawrence, owner of the shop. 'How we have suffered,' Kathleen says, recalling prison terms and hunger strikes. I sense a sympathy in Marie, alongside a belief that this is how tragedy must play out.

A few months later Marie finds another opportunity to visit Cork. Back in the hardware shop, she spies Lawrence, and before she can prepare herself, is ushered into his tiny office.

'He is a small man, aged sixty-five, with a bad tremor in his right hand and arm. His right eye is false and from time to time his mouth has a remarkable twist to the left. He is old for his years, which is not surprising for one who went through all the troubled times on active service,' she writes. In 1920 he had been seventeen years old and a member of the Fianna. Just four years older than Marie.

Believing she is writing a book about the period, he talks fluently about his experiences, offering her the chance to photograph his gun and the bullet that passed through his jaw. As a long-term republican he regrets 'more wasn't done during the struggle'. Later, when she brings up Sergeant O'Donoghue's shooting, he indicates he was one of the three gunmen. He also provides the reason why – random chance. On that November evening the three men had been awaiting another man who did not show up. They were about to abandon the mission when they spotted my grandfather. One of them thought he was on their list so they might as well get him. All three fired.

Marie writes: 'My face must have registered horror, for Lawrence continued: "It sounds horrible, awful, but we did not think so at the time. It was just part of the day's job."'

If James had walked by five minutes later, he might have survived. Their might-have-been life passes before her.

As she prepares to leave, she knows he will offer to shake hands. This is a major hurdle.

'How often had I told God in prayer that I forgave them, and always I had the sneaking feeling that if I met one of them face to face, I would turn away ... He had his back to the door ... I stood up to go. He opened the door for me and held out his hand. I took it, but who can tell my feelings? ... I left him at 5.40 p.m. It had taken me forty-eight years to get the names.'

Later she wonders if he hasn't guessed who she was.

My aunt made a last pilgrimage to Cork in 1973. The hardware shop had been sold. Lawrence was dead, as was Kathleen. 'So all involved in my father's murder have now gone to face their God,' she writes. What she doesn't mention is her personal sorrow. My own father, her closest ally, was also dead. She was to live fifteen years after him. Always, I think, an orphan.

It's over one hundred years since my grandfather was killed, almost as long since my grandmother died. The heroes of the independence struggle are gone and my own generation are beginning to disappear. Marie herself is buried in the graveyard of her convent, where few present-day nuns remain. Many of the ideals she gave her life to are in decline. I can't say whether the answers she found from her quest brought her peace of mind, but I salute her purpose and her intention to forgive.

This is a partial account that weaves together three generations. Following the fashion of our time, I feel that Marie's own story should be preserved, but I'm conscious of the unspoken in this and all narrative, and my present-day biases. The reasons Uncle Michael bound Marie and my father to silence were strong and valid. Too often violence leads to a spiral of killing, leaving shadows that can stunt the people who have to live their lives in the aftermath, like my aunt. I picture her as a lone black figure waving us goodbye from the convent door. A faithful survivor.

Nessa O'Mahony

AFTERWORD
CICATRICE – THE SCAR HEALED?

In 1989, Eavan Boland published an essay in which she set
out her ideas about the position of the woman poet in
Ireland. Titled *A Kind of Scar*, and published as the first of
Attic Press's LIP pamphlets on 'contemporary issues and
controversies, by Irish women writers, thinkers and
activists', Eavan began the essay by describing a visit to
Achill Island she had undertaken one Easter many years
before, when she was still a young college student at
Trinity. Whilst staying in a cottage there, Eavan had
encountered the caretaker, an elderly local woman who
told her many stories about what happened on the island
during the Famine years; these were stories of death and
survival, how the villagers at Keel had moved closer to the
seashore to be better able to eat the seaweed.

Eavan questioned why she knew so little of this history,
despite coming from the same culture and shared past.
Why was she studying English court poetry, and not the

experiences of women such as this? Why was there no place for women's experience in the Irish poetic tradition, other than being the subject of it in tropes like Dark Rosaleen or Cathleen Ní Houlihan? Where were the poetic foremothers, the Irish women writers, in whose tradition she might follow?

And whilst there certainly were Irish women poets writing in the decades preceding Eavan's arrival on the scene – one thinks of Rhoda Coghill, Sheila Wingfield and Freda Laughton, to name but a few – they had not entered the canon in a way in which a young student like Eavan Boland might have encountered them. In the essay she says:

> Irish poetry was predominantly male ... now and again, in discussion, you heard a woman's name. But the lived vocation, the craft witnessed by a human life – that was missing. And I missed it. Not in the beginning, perhaps. But later, when perceptions of womanhood began to redirect my own work, what I regretted was the absence of an expressed poetic life which would have dignified and revealed mine.

Thus, when under the influence of American feminist poets such as Adrienne Rich, Eavan began to publish her own, deeply personal, poetry of female experience, she encountered some critical backlash. Collections such as *In Her Own Image* and *Night Feed* were dismissed, in some quarters, as second-rate – Boland herself talked about hearing a male poet query at a reading whether she was still 'peddling that menstrual poetry'. It took decades before the idea that women's poetry was somehow inferior to dissipate into the ether.

It is fair to say that there has also been some academic pushback to Eavan's argument that she lacked poetic foremothers. Critics have pointed to the significant number of women poets who were in fact successfully publishing in journals and book form in the first half of the twentieth century – poets who are now once more to be found in new editions and translations – and questioned why Eavan seemed determined to ignore anyone who might have undermined her own argument about being so solitary a writer in a predominantly male environment. But there's a big difference between the existence of women writers during that period, and general awareness of them afterwards in terms of their place within the canon. In that pre-internet age, access to information was limited and women poets fell out of print, and far away from the canon, very easily. It is certainly true that Eavan's Arlen House collections, *The War Horse* (1980), *In Her Own Image* (1980), *Night Feed* (1982), and *The Journey and Other Poems* (1986), were published on a scale unlike any Irish woman poet before her, in print runs of many thousands, with national and international distribution, and widespread marketing and media campaigns.

If Eavan was writing about her experiences in the 1960s, the situation had not changed twenty years later when I was a student. When I studied literature in University College Dublin, there were still few women writers on the curriculum. I do remember we studied Maria Edgeworth and Emily Dickinson, but when we entered the twentieth century, the reading lists were determinedly masculine, set with great confidence and conviction by a predominantly male faculty. If there was a living, breathing source of women writers whose texts we might study, they weren't sharing that information in the tile-floored corridors of Belfield. The fact that the three *E*'s – Eithne Strong, Eiléan Ní Chuilleanáin and Eavan Boland – were already well-published Irish women poets when I was studying literature was neither here nor there.

So one can hardly blame Eavan for her lack of awareness two decades earlier. But her perspective was very much to look forward rather than back and there was a job of work to be done in creating a better environment for women who wanted to write. In *A Kind of Scar* she stated that her central premise was that 'over a relatively short time – certainly no more than a generation or so – women have moved from being the subjects and objects of Irish poems to being the authors of them.' For her, this was a 'momentous' and 'disruptive' transit which 'changes our idea of the Irish poem; of its composition and authority, of its right to appropriate certain themes and make certain fiats'. It made perfect sense to her to work to facilitate that transit in any way she could, and the writing workshop, accessible to women the length and breadth of Ireland, was the perfect vehicle for such activism.

It's hard to overestimate the impact her teaching and facilitation had on women writers. When the Women's Education Bureau (WEB) was founded by Catherine Rose in 1984, and Eavan appointed Creative Director, she gathered, for the first time, a range of resources aimed at developing new Irish women writers. These included numerous events islandwide, the Writers and Readers' Day at the National Gallery, and the Annual Writers' Workshop for Women, in which many prominent women writers took their first steps. Writing about the experience from a participant's point of view, Liz McManus told me:

> I remember being overawed by being in a group of women writers. Until then I had felt completely alone and lacking in confidence. I remember Eavan mentioning that she was more comfortable critiquing poetry than prose and I realised I wasn't the only one outside their comfort zone. When Ivy [Bannister] suggested to me after that last workshop ended that we should keep meeting, I was so delighted not to have to go back to isolation again.

Writing in *Poetry Ireland Review* 138, the special tribute issue to Eavan Boland, poet Catherine Phil MacCarthy spoke of a writing workshop she attended with Eavan in 1987 in Dundrum in south Dublin, an adult education evening class attended by some twenty-six people.

MacCarthy describes listening to Eavan discuss the practical craft of poetry, but also the political environment that had led to the omission of so many women from contemporary anthologies. Eavan showed MacCarthy a path along which she might find her own way, a path that began in a teacher-student relationship and which developed into mentorship and friendship. In the same issue, Jean O'Brien described a similar evolution, noting that in early workshops with her, Eavan had noted how 'the men put their work forward with aplomb, but the women put theirs shyly out after persuasion' and concluded by advising O'Brien that she 'needed to learn from the men', a lesson that Jean never forgot in terms of 'clearing a space' for herself in the world of poetry.

It is impossible to quantify the number of women writers Eavan inspired over the years, on either side of the Atlantic. Her move to Stanford provided opportunities for generations of young American writers to learn from her. But it is clear that her very presence, both as a teacher and a writer and an essayist, was hugely influential and helped to change the environment for so many of us.

If Eavan's workshops were an important strand to her literary activism, so too was her desire to refocus attention on already forgotten Irish women writers. Writing in *Poetry Ireland Review* 138, publisher Alan Hayes reminded us that as early as 1978, when Eavan herself began working at Arlen House, she started a campaign to revivify the reputations of dead women writers, and to build reputations and careers for emerging ones. In 1978 Arlen House announced a national competition for female debut short story writers, with Boland, Mary Lavin and David Marcus as judges. Eavan edited and introduced the book, *The Wall Reader*, Ireland's first anthology of women fiction writers (which became an unexpected No. 1 bestseller for many weeks in summer 1979), despite a media backlash, from both male and female critics who said there wasn't a need for a female-only competition and anthology.

And in 1979, Eavan and Arlen House announced a classic literature series, the first title of which was Kate O'Brien's *The Ante-Room*, with a preface by Eavan herself. O'Brien's work was largely out of print at this point, and her major contribution to Irish writing in danger of being forgotten. The work done by Arlen House, both through publication and through the establishment of the Kate O'Brien Weekend in Limerick four years later, helped to re-establish her position in the canon. Other writers included in the classic literature series were Janet McNeill, Anne Crone, Katherine Keane and Norah Hoult.

I was of a later generation to Eavan. When I made my first tentative steps into the world of literature in the mid-1990s, I began to discover that not only were there living, breathing women writers out there, they were in plentiful supply in Ireland. Their words could be found in pamphlets, collections, the occasional anthology. And even if some of those anthologies had to be published to redress the balance of the absence of women in other anthologies, they were still providing opportunities for me, and others like me, to get myself heard. In the mid-1990s, for example, I first encountered Denis Collins and Anne Heffernan at the Wexford Arts Centre, and discovered their passion project, *Women's Work*, a series of books foregrounding the writing of women from all over the island of Ireland. Their National Women's Poetry Competition was an important platform for many of us at the beginning of our careers. So too was Joan McBreen's enormously important anthology *The White Page* published by Salmon Poetry in 1999, which featured a comprehensive list of women poets, all of whom had published at least one volume. Eavan was one of Salmon's earliest supporters and contributors, and

Salmon continues its leadership role and sterling work in developing women's writing in Ireland and internationally.

But although we were beginning to publish our work, we weren't very good at articulating our poetic process. I first encountered Eavan Boland through her prose – her essay collection *Object Lessons* – not her poetry, and was shocked that a woman might write so seriously about her own poetics, be so concerned with her own position as a poet and a woman in Ireland. I might have accepted it from a Heaney or a Muldoon, but if publishing poetry had begun to be women's work, the writing about one's own poetry, the articulation of a poetic aesthetic, still seemed to me to be man's work – a woman positioning herself in such a way seemed unseemly! The hard conditioning of a third-level education in Irish literature had yet to wear off.

But as ever, with poetry, the cure for such lack of awareness is to read, and to listen. I remember attending a reading of Eavan's in Dublin in the late 1990s – I think it must have been around the publication of her collection *The Lost Land*. The venue was the Royal Irish Academy on Dawson Street, and Eavan's reading was typically lucid, precise and provoking. When the reading had ended, the crowd gathered for the book signing, and yet I felt there was a distance between us and the poet who had engrossed us over the previous forty minutes. Shyness, perhaps, or diffidence, on both sides. We hadn't yet learned how to read this poet, this woman whose purpose had a seriousness we didn't know how to navigate, used as we were to the hail-fellow-well-met smiling public men of Irish poetry.

Still I didn't know her, and wouldn't have done, had my friend and colleague Siobhán Campbell not approached me with the idea for a scholarly work she'd long been planning – a book of essays responding to Eavan in the context of the poet's seventieth birthday. Incredibly, such a work had not yet been produced, in Ireland or elsewhere. Siobhán wanted to fill the vacuum, and we had little difficulty persuading the poets and scholars we approached to write a response. The project gave me a reason to read everything Eavan had written, and to finally understand the consistency of her vision. To my deep surprise I shared some of her obsessions. Although my political awareness was still blunted, as a student of history I could respond to her preoccupations with what history can teach us, and more importantly, how the omissions from the historical record needed to be put right.

We didn't consult with Eavan during the production of *Eavan Boland: Inside History*, but it was important to us that she be happy with the concept, and her demeanour on the night it was launched, two years after her seventieth birthday, at a crammed Poetry Ireland, indicated that she was. The reserved, serious person I'd first seen nearly two decades earlier had been replaced by a smiling, approachable woman who had time for everyone there to celebrate a lifetime's achievement. And she took nothing for granted. As the evening drifted into night, and she was still surrounded by fans and well-wishers, I felt that my job had been done and I was ready to leave. As I was going out the door, I heard her voice behind me, calling me back. She'd wanted to tell me how grateful she was to Siobhán and I for the work we'd done. I stuttered back how grateful we were for the work she'd done, for us, and for women writers everywhere.

Our paths crossed a few times after that – she'd taken on the role of editor of *Poetry Ireland Review* and attended many of the launches of the journal during that time. It felt as if she had embraced the Irish poetry scene as warmly as it was embracing her, after decades of shyness and distance. Under her editorship, the journal became a more inclusive and diverse space – each issue introduced new names and shook our assumptions of what Irish poetry was, or should be.

Then in the summer of 2017, I was asked to undertake a public interview with Eavan in London. The prestigious Irish Literary Society was hosting the London launch of *Eavan Boland: Inside History,* and Eavan had graciously agreed to be interviewed at the event. I was to be the interviewer.

That might have been reason enough for the nerves to flutter as I walked up the steps of the Bloomsbury Hotel. In fact I was quite sanguine at the prospect of conducting a public interview. I'd done my research, prepared my questions, and was fairly confident that I would acquit myself well. No, what was bothering me now was the suggestion I'd made some weeks earlier that Eavan and I should have a cup of tea to chat before the event, an invitation she'd graciously accepted. And whilst I'd met her several times before at poetry events, I'd never actually spent any time alone in her company. The social responsibility was terrifying.

I'd googled suitable places close to the Bloomsbury Hotel, where the interview was to take place, and had found one that seemed eminently appropriate. Tea and Tattle was a tea room over an antiquarian bookshop and was resplendent with mahogany tables groaning under tiered bone-china cake stands and an eclectic mix of Crown Derby tea cups and saucers. I arrived first, Eavan shortly afterwards, and there followed a simply delightful sixty minutes of chat, and not much solemnity at all. The incisiveness so many have commented upon was there, but the overall tenor was warm and witty, light and companionable.

One of the topics that came up during that hour of chat was the notion of anthologies and canon-creation. I still recall the flash of steel that entered Eavan's eyes when she mentioned the infamous *Field Day Anthology* which had managed to exclude so many women writers from its curation of centuries of Irish literature – Eavan was one of the very few Irish women included. For her, the *Field Day* farrago was just another example of how tightly the gatekeepers had grasped the padlocks, and was reason enough for her lifelong concern to take a bolt cutter to those locks and barriers, and to open the doors to all-comers.

There is no longer question about the place of the woman writer in contemporary Irish literature – there hasn't been for some time now. That's not to say that there aren't other types of exclusions; writers of colour regularly point to the lack of opportunities in writing, reviewing, editing and curating. So there is no room for complacency, nor would I suggest that there's anything remotely resembling a level playing field in terms of class or ethnicity. And we must not forget that progress can be halted and reversed. But Eavan Boland's work as a writer and teacher gives us a template for how we can respond to other omissions, and to keep the doors open to all who would wish to gain entry.

IVY BANNISTER has published collections of stories and poems, and a memoir. Her radio work includes plays, stories and many short essays. She has won the Hennessy Award, the Francis MacManus Award, the O.Z. Whitehead Drama Award, and the Best Short Poetry Collection and Best Play Awards in Listowel. It's rumoured that she cooks the finest lasagne in South County Dublin.

SHEILA BARRETT is the author of two published novels, *Walk in a Lost Landscape* and *A View to Die For.* Her short stories have appeared in a number of anthologies and have been broadcast on radio. All this began after she attended Eavan Boland's workshop in Dundrum. Arlen House published her first short story in *The Adultery* in 1982.

LOUISE C. CALLAGHAN is the author of five books of poetry. She has been published in the *Field Day Anthology of Irish Literature, Vols IV* and *V.* Her work is recorded in the UCD Irish Poetry Reading Archive. A play called *Find the Lady,* based on the life of Kate O'Brien, was commissioned by the Abbey Theatre (1993). *Moonlight: A Full Moon,* her recent collection, is the subject of a conversation on the podcast *Books for Breakfast.*

MARY ROSE CALLAGHAN was born in Ireland in 1944 and emigrated to the United States in 1975, where she lived for many years. She was a winner in the first Arlen House short story competition. As a result, her first novel, *Mothers,* was published. She has written eight more novels, some of which have been translated into German and Danish, and was an assistant editor of *The Dictionary of Irish Literature.* She is also a playwright and biographer, and an award-winning short story writer. Her memoir, *The Deep End,* will be published in Ireland in 2023 by Sweeney & O'Donovan.

SUSAN CONNOLLY lives in Drogheda, County Louth. Her poetry collections include *For the Stranger* (Dedalus Press, 1993), *Forest Music* (Shearsman Books, 2009) and *Bridge of the Ford* (Shearsman Books, 2016). She was awarded the Patrick and Katherine Kavanagh Fellowship in Poetry in 2001. Her poems are in *The Field Day Anthology, Voices and Poetry of Ireland* and *Windharp*.

COLETTE CONNOR completed a BA in English studies and an MPhil in creative writing at TCD. She also has an MA in women's studies from UCD. Shortlisted for a Hennessy Award, her poems have been published in Ireland and abroad. A collection of poems, short stories and a novel, *The Chateau Fort*, await a publisher. She also studies at NCAD.

CATHERINE DUNNE is the author of prize-winning novels and one work of non-fiction, *An Unconsidered People* (2003/2021), exploring the lives of Irish immigrants in 1950s London. Her novels have been shortlisted for the Novel of the Year at the Irish Book Awards, at Listowel Writers' Week, and for the International Strega Prize for fiction. Catherine received the Irish PEN Award in 2018.

PHILOMENA FEIGHAN won her first short story prize at fifteen. She was shortlisted for the Hennessy Awards, won the fiction prize at Listowel Writers' Week and an Ian St James Award. On moving to Massachusetts, she earned an MFA and completed a novel, an extract of which won an Evvy Award for Best Prose.

CELIA DE FRÉINE writes in Irish and English. Poetry awards include the Patrick Kavanagh Award and Gradam Litríochta Chló Iar-Chonnacht. Her screenplays have won awards in Ireland and America and her plays have won Oireachtas awards. She has been shortlisted three times for the An Post Book Awards. *Aoi ag Bord na Teanga* (*Leabhair*COMHAR) is her most recent book.

SHAUNA GILLIGAN has been a member of WEB for over five years. Her short fiction has been widely published. She's received many accolades for writing including a Cecil Day Lewis Award (2015) and a Brigid 1500 Arts and Creativity Grant (2023, Kildare County Council). Her most recent book is *Mantles* (Arlen House, 2021), a collaboration with visual artist Margo McNulty. shaunagilliganwriter.com

ANTONIA HART recently completed a PhD in history at Trinity College. Her book *Ghost Signs of Dublin* was published in 2014. She lives in Dún Laoghaire.

PHYL HERBERT is from Dublin and since retiring from her teaching career completed an MPhil in creative writing in 2008. Her debut collection of short stories, *After Desire*, was published by Arlen House in 2016. Her memoir, *The Price of Silence* (working title), will be published by Sweeney & O'Donovan.

PATRICIA HICKEY is a novelist and short story writer. She was born in Dublin and worked with Aer Lingus prior to attending college. She is a sociology and politics graduate of Trinity College. She is a founder member and National Secretary of the National Parents Council (Primary). She has broadcast short stories and been a guest reviewer on radio. She lives in North County Dublin with her husband, Martin. They have three children and five grandchildren.

JOAN LEECH is a retired second-level teacher of English, French and Spanish. She has had work published several times, including poetry and short stories. Originally from Buncrana, a small seaside town close to the border in County Donegal, she now lives in Navan, County Meath, with Penny, her Jack Russell.

ANTOINETTE McCARTHY was shortlisted for the Francis MacManus RTÉ Short Story Competition in 2022 for the second time. She has also been shortlisted for the Over the

Edge Short Story Competition and the Lilliput Press Culture Night Short Story Competition. Her story, 'We've Probably Missed the Waving' was published in *Crannóg* in 2022.

ANN MCKAY has lived in the city on the Foyle in Northern Ireland for most of her life. Her first poetry collection, *Giving Shine*, was published by Summer Palace Press in 2000. In 2021 she and performance artist/poet James King self-published *Parley Palaver*, a collection of poems and drawings.

MARILYN MCLAUGHLIN was born in 1951 in Derry and studied English and German at Trinity College. She then taught, acted, attended art classes and freelanced at the Verbal Arts Centre, Guildhall Press and Radio Foyle. She joined writing groups, wrote short stories and poems, sometimes won prizes, sometimes published – not all at the same time! And she recently got an MA in poetry at Queens in Belfast.

LIZ MCMANUS is a novelist and former parliamentarian. A founder member of WEB, her books are *Acts of Subversion* (1991), *A Shadow in the Yard* (2015) and *When Things Come to Light* (2023). She has won the Hennessy award for New Irish Writing, the Listowel Short Story and Irish PEN awards. She was awarded an MPhil in 2012. She is working on a PhD in creative writing.

LIA MILLS writes novels, short stories, literary essays and memoir. Her novel, *Fallen*, was the Dublin/Belfast Two Cities One Book selection in 2016. A new edition of her first novel, *Another Alice*, was published in 2022 as part of the Arlen House Classic Literature series. A mentor on the National Mentoring Programme, she is currently working on her fourth novel.

SARA MULLEN has been a member of WEB since 2015. Originally from Castlebar, County Mayo, she lives in Dublin, where she works as an English teacher. She holds an MPhil in creative writing from the Oscar Wilde Centre, Trinity College, and her poetry and short fiction have featured in various publications in Ireland and beyond. She won first prize in the 2019 Ballyroan Library Poetry Competition.

PATSY J. MURPHY was born in England in 1941 but spent her early childhood with her grandfather in Dublin. She studied at UCD and thr New University of Ulster and worked as a production assistant in RTÉ television drama department in the sixties. She lived in Paris and was a Fulbright Scholar at the New School for Social Research, New York. She lectured in Institutes of Technology in Donegal, Dublin and Galway.

ÉILÍS NÍ DHUIBHNE was born in Dublin in 1954. She is a founding member of the WEB Writers' Group, having attended the National Women Writers' Workshop in 1985. Since then she has published more than thirty books. Her most recent books are *Twelve Thousand Days: A Memoir* (shortlisted for the Michel Déon Award 2020), *Little Red and Other Stories* (Blackstaff, 2020), and (ed.), *Look! It's a Woman Writer!: Irish Literary Feminisms 1970–2020* (Arlen House, 2021). She is a recipient of the PEN Award for an Outstanding Contribution to Irish Literature, and a Hennessy Hall of Fame Award. She is a member of Aosdána and President of the Folklore of Ireland Society.

HELENA NOLAN is a Patrick Kavanagh Award winner and was shortlisted for the Hennessy, Strokestown and FISH awards. She holds an MA in creative writing from UCD and is widely published in anthologies and journals, including in *Washing Windows II & III* and *Poetry Ireland Review*. As Irish Ambassador to Belgium and now as Consul General in New York, she maintains a focus on cultural diplomacy and support for Irish writers and artists. Helena is co-editor of *All Strangers Here: 100 Years of Personal Writing from the Irish Foriegn Service*.

CLAIRR O'CONNOR, a poet, playwright and fiction writer, has written five collections of poetry: *When You Need Them* (1989), *Breast* (2004), *Trick the Lock* (2008), *So Far* (2012) and *Caesura* (2017). Her novels are *Belonging* (1991), *Love in Another Room* (1995) and *Finding Home* (2020). Her radio plays have been broadcast by BBC Radio 4, RTÉ Radio 1 and Radio Warsaw.

MARY O'DONNELL is a writer of fiction, poetry, short stories, non-fiction and essays. Her work has been published widely, and includes four novels, among them the critically acclaimed *Where They Lie,* the subject of which is the 'disappeared' in the North of Ireland, as well as recent poetry, *Massacre of the Birds*. A limited edition chapbook is forthcoming from Southword Editions in autumn 2023. She lectures, gives talks, facilitates workshops and writes journalism. Her work is translated into Portuguese, Spanish and Hungarian. She is a member of Aosdána.

BETH O'HALLORAN is a visual artist and lecturer at the National College of Art and Design. Publications include *Litbreak* 2022, *Brooklyn* Vol. 1 and *The Ogham Stone* 2020. Twice shortlisted for the Hennessy New Irish Writing Award, in 2019 'Vortex' was awarded *The Irish Times* First Fiction Award.

NESSA O'MAHONY is from Dublin. She has published five collections of poetry, the most recent being *The Hollow Woman on the Island* (Salmon Poetry, 2019). She has edited/co-edited various anthologies, including, with Siobhán Campbell, *Eavan Boland: Inside History* (Arlen House, 2017). In 2022 she was guest editor of *Poetry Ireland Review,* Issue 138, a special tribute issue to Eavan Boland.

ANNE ROPER is a writer and documentary maker.

SUSAN SCHREIBMAN is Professor of Digital Arts and Culture at Maastricht University. She has published poems in a number of journals over the past thirty years.

Monica Strina is a native of Sardinia, Italy, who has fallen in love with Ireland and now lives in Dublin with her twin boys and lovely dog. She studied foreign languages and literature and has a master's degree in creative writing. Monica has a passion for literary fiction and finds it hard to go anywhere without a book. Her other passions are yoga, baking, hiking and good food.

Breda Wall Ryan lives in Bray, County Wicklow. Internationally published and anthologised, her many awards include the Gregory O'Donoghue International Poetry Prize and Dermot Healy International Poetry Award. A founding member of Hibernian Poetry, her collections are *In a Hare's Eye* (Shine/Strong Award 2016), and *Raven Mothers* (2018). Her third collection is due in late 2023.

Dolores Walshe's awards include two Arts Council bursaries, the Berlin Writing Prize, the Bryan MacMahon Award, the O.Z. Whitehead/PEN Playwriting Award, and the Irish Stage and Screen Playwriting Award. She was awarded second prize (twice) by the Francis MacManus Short Story Competition. She has had a novel and short story collection published by Wolfhound Press. Her plays have been staged by the Royal Exchange Theatre, Manchester and Andrew's Lane Theatre, Dublin, and are published by Syracuse University Press and Carysfort Press.

Máiríde Woods writes poetry and short stories. Her work has appeared in anthologies and reviews. She has won two Hennessy Awards and the Francis MacManus Short Story Award. Three poetry collections have been published by Astrolabe, including *A Constant Elsewhere of the Mind* in 2017. Máiríde was brought up in Cushendall, County Antrim, but has spent most of her life in North Dublin.

ACKNOWLEDGEMENTS

Quotes from *Poetry Ireland Review,* Issue 138 (December 2022) in Nessa O'Mahony's essays are courtesy of Poetry Ireland.

The extract from Sheila Wingfield's poem 'Waking' from *Collected Poems 1938–1983,* is courtesy of Hill and Wang, New York.

The image of Eavan Boland at Annaghmakerrig convening the Annual Writers' Workshop for Women is courtesy of Icebox Films.

We gratefully acknowledge the financial support of dlr Libraries and Creative Ireland in making this anthology possible.